THIS IS HAR[

Praise for the

It was only a matter of time before a clever publisher realized that there is an audience for whom *Exile on Main Street* or *Electric Ladyland* are as significant and worthy of study as *The Catcher in the Rye* or *Middlemarch* ... The series ... is freewheeling and eclectic, ranging from minute rock-geek analysis to idiosyncratic personal celebration — *The New York Times Book Review*

Ideal for the rock geek who thinks liner notes just aren't enough — *Rolling Stone*

One of the coolest publishing imprints on the planet — *Bookslut*

These are for the insane collectors out there who appreciate fantastic design, well-executed thinking, and things that make your house look cool. Each volume in this series takes a seminal album and breaks it down in startling minutiae. We love these. We are huge nerds — *Vice*

A brilliant series ... each one a work of real love — *NME* (UK)

Passionate, obsessive, and smart — *Nylon*

Religious tracts for the rock 'n' roll faithful — *Boldtype*

[A] consistently excellent series — *Uncut* (UK)

We ... aren't naive enough to think that we're your only source for reading about music (but if we had our way ... watch out). For those of you who really like to know everything there is to know about an album, you'd do well to check out Bloomsbury's "33 1/3" series of books — *Pitchfork*

For almost 20 years, the 33-and-a-Third series of music books has focused on individual albums by acts well known (Bob Dylan, Nirvana, Abba, Radiohead), cultish (Neutral Milk Hotel, Throbbing Gristle, Wire) and many levels in-between. The range of music and their creators defines "eclectic", while the writing veers from freewheeling to acutely insightful. In essence, the books are for the music fan who (as Rolling Stone noted) "thinks liner notes just aren't enough." — *The Irish Times*

For reviews of individual titles in the series, please visit our blog at 333sound.com and our website at https://www.bloomsbury.com/academic/music-sound-studies/

Follow us on Twitter: @333books

Like us on Facebook: https://www.facebook.com/33.3books

For a complete list of books in this series, see the back of this book.

Forthcoming in the series:

Shout at the Devil by Micco Caporale
101 by Mary Valle
White Limozeen by Steacy Easton
I'm Wide Awake, It's Morning by Holden Seidlitz
Hounds of Love by Leah Kardos
Re by Carmelo Esterrich
New Amerykah Part Two (Return of the Ankh)
by Kameryn Alexa Carter
In the Life of Chris Gaines by Stephen Deusner

and many more...

This Is Hardcore

Jane Savidge

BLOOMSBURY ACADEMIC
NEW YORK • LONDON • OXFORD • NEW DELHI • SYDNEY

BLOOMSBURY ACADEMIC

Bloomsbury Publishing Inc
1385 Broadway, New York, NY 10018, USA
50 Bedford Square, London, WC1B 3DP, UK
29 Earlsfort Terrace, Dublin 2, Ireland

BLOOMSBURY, BLOOMSBURY ACADEMIC and the Diana logo are
trademarks of Bloomsbury Publishing Plc
First published in the United States of America 2024

A catalog record for this book is available from the Library of Congress.

ISBN: PB: 979-8-7651-0695-2
       ePDF: 979-8-7651-0697-6
       eBook: 979-8-7651-0696-9

Series: 33 1/3

Typeset by RefineCatch Limited, Bungay, Suffolk
Printed and bound in Great Britain

To find out more about our authors and books visit www.bloomsbury.com
and sign up for our newsletters.

For Steve Mackey

Contents

Prelude: Fame: What Is It Good For?   x

1   You Got to Take These Dreams and Make
    Them Whole   1
2   Something Changed   13
3   This Is the Eye of the Storm   23
4   That Goes in There   31
5   The Sound of Someone Losing the Plot   41
6   The Earth Is Where We Are   51
7   Nightclubbing   55
8   Leave Your Wheelchair Outside   61
9   This Is Barry   67
10 A Hangover without End   77
11 Letters Home   83
12 Cartoons From Other People's Lives   91
13 Let's Get It On   97
14 You Look Like Her to Me   103
15 Come Share This Golden Age with Me   107

CONTENTS

16 The Meek Shall Inherit Absolutely Nothing at All   113
17 "Are you well? Well, you won't be in a minute."   119

Postlude: The Sound of Failure   123
Notes   127
Acknowledgements   135

Prelude
Fame: What Is It Good For?

"Good afternoon. Total Fame Solutions. How may I direct your call?"

"Hello, I wonder if you can help me. I have become famous by mistake. Well, not by mistake exactly, as I'd always thought I'd be famous. It's just that . . . the reality of fame has turned out to be something entirely different to what I thought it might turn out to be."

There is a pause.

"I'm sorry, I am not sure I understand what you are asking me. Are you saying that you need some assistance with the level of fame you have currently attained? Because, if so, we have a whole range of package deals that might easily satisfy your requirements!"

There is a sigh from our valiant champion. Indeed, this is how he'd envisaged the conversation would turn out: like an informal chat with a virtual assistant masquerading as a real-life customer service representative for a ludicrously-named corporation of indeterminate expediency.

"Look, I don't know why I'm calling you, but I got your number off someone who used to work for me, and he seemed to think you'd be able to help. The thing is, I wanted to be a pop

star from the age of eleven or twelve, and I had this idea that I could actually be an astronaut and a pop star at the same time. And if I could combine the two careers – and overcome my shyness with girls – it would just make things easier."

At this point, he lets out a slightly more exasperated, if ever-more-gentle, sigh.

"Me and my band, Pulp, recorded our first John Peel Session in 1981, but it took another twelve years before anyone had really heard of us, and then another two before we became everyone's favourite new indie band. And then, barely a few months later, my life spiralled completely out of control. There was an incident. . .with Michael Jackson."

"An incident? With Michael Jackson? That does sound very interesting, and it does sound like the level of fame you have currently attained is proving to be somewhat problematic. As I mentioned, we do offer a wide range of services and deals, but we are primarily focused on providing security services to the rich and famous, and those that are threatened by their fame. We have been in business for over thirty years now, and we've never had any complaints."

One has to admit that this was a pretty impressive track record. But this is beside the point.

"If we can just stick to the subject for the moment, I have to tell you that, from childhood, I knew that human beings have to believe in something. In the absence of religion, I believed in the dream, and I think it performed that function, especially when I was living in fairly shitty circumstances. I think that's also why, when Pulp became famous, I didn't like fame. Getting famous was supposed to be like going to heaven. But you don't get to go to heaven while you're still alive. There was no way on

earth it was ever going to match up to what I'd imagined it to be, so inevitably it was a crushing disappointment." There is another pause, since this is proving to be more difficult than our caller had imagined. *"And anyway, I don't know why I am telling you all this. I need to speak to an expert. Are you an expert?"*

"No, I am not an expert," replies the customer service representative, with ill-disguised disdain, *"but thank you for affording me the courtesy of enquiring as to whether I could be of service to you in that regard. I am sensing that you are enduring a level of inner conflict that none of us here at the front desk, or within our regular Services Department, are qualified to deal with. So, I am going to transfer you to our Philosophy Department. We are currently experiencing a high number of calls, but bear with me."*

Philosophy Department? The line appears to go dead, if not for a low drone that sounds like the start of a new Pulp song called, 'Seductive Barry'. And then, after a moment, another voice comes on the line.

"Hello, you're through to the TFS Philosophy Department. How may I resolve your conflict?"

"Erm, I was just telling your customer service representative that being a popstar was the thing I wanted to do my whole life. And then actually becoming a popstar was the culmination of my ambition. But I didn't like it! I kind of allowed myself to go along with it, thinking, 'This is it! You've got a career now.' And now I'm here, and I don't know what to do!"

"Ah, yes, the inadequacies and disappointments of fame!" says the voice, rather too dismissively for our caller's liking. *Could it be that they are not taking his enquiries entirely*

seriously? Or is he just one popstar in a long line of popstars that day having trouble finding their inner truth? Only time would be able to tell.

"*You are no doubt familiar with the expression, 'Self-consciousness attains its self-consciousness in another self-consciousness,*'" says the voice. "*It's a quotation from Hegel, of course, but perhaps it applies most particularly in your case. After all, our very identity requires the eyes of others, and it's impossible to change the world without first being recognised by other people. And it sounds like you really wanted to change the world?*"

Our caller thinks about this for a moment. *These people are really rather good*, he says to himself.

"*Look,*" says our caller, "*Making Pulp's new album, 'This Is Hardcore', has been almost overwhelmingly weird. I'm in this place where I'm not that happy, and it was making a record that did it, so why make another one? But part of being in a pop band was, 'I want to be famous,' and I did want that. I think that's quite a common thing in our society – this idea that being famous is going to sort things out for you before it inevitably doesn't. There's been so many films made about that, you would think we'd have got the message. I had to extricate that from the genuine desire to actually create things.*"

"*Let me stop you there,*" says the voice, "*because I want to tell you that you are not alone. Years from now, there's going to be an entire industry devoted to the sort of issues we are talking about today. Total Fame Solutions are very much pioneers in this rapidly-expanding arena of public-private conflict – and you are lucky to have found us.*" At this point, our celebrated adventurer begins to wonder whether he has stumbled upon another virtual assistant, although admittedly, one of a slightly higher calibre. But then the voice continues, *"One day, Brad Pitt – you may have seen him in 'Seven' and '12 Monkeys'? – will be self-assured enough to admit that 'Fame makes you feel permanently like a girl walking past construction workers.' And a popstar called Lady Gaga – who is only twelve years old as I speak! – will one day confess to all and sundry, 'I don't think I could think of a single thing that's more isolating than being famous.' And that's before you consider a further roll call of yet-to-be-famous, future celebrities like Katy Perry, who may go on to say, 'Fame is just a disgusting by-product of what I do', or Jennifer Lawrence – she's barely eight years old as we discuss these matters – suggesting, 'If I were just your average twenty-three-year-old girl, and I called the police to say that there were strange men sleeping on my lawn, and following me to Starbucks, they would leap into action.' Sounds familiar? Of course it does! Welcome to Total Fame Solutions!"*

This was getting ridiculous. On the one hand, our swashbuckling idol is in the actual process of talking to someone from the Philosophy Department of a company called Total Fame Solutions – for heaven's sake! – who seem to be claiming that they know the intimate details of conversations that yet-to-be famous celebrities are going to have with the worldwide media! And on the other hand, here he is again, presented with the kind of platitudes and inanities that have no doubt arrived on his doorstep courtesy of the absurd state of affairs that have gotten him here in the first place. Perhaps he has now become marooned in the Platitudes and Inanities Department of Total Fame Solutions by mistake?

"Tell me about your parents," says the voice. *"Did you have a good relationship with your mother? Did you have a good relationship with your father? Could either of them have facilitated your initial interest in fame and your ongoing relationship with it thereafter? Have you lost a parent?"*

Classic, thinks our audacious interlocutor. *Bring the parents into it! Blame them! That'll do it! And I'm paying good money for this? Come to think of it, I have no idea who's paying for this. Perhaps, it's my management? Or the record company? I can't remember.*

"I really don't want to talk about my mother and father," says our caller. *"They have nothing to do with it."*

"On the contrary," says the voice. *"They have everything to do with it. Losing a parent in whatever circumstances – and I understand your father left the marital home when you were seven years old? – is like losing the audience to our lives. Parents give us our first taste of fame. From infancy, most of us are fawned over in our every step, smile, and stumble. We become accustomed to the idea that someone will always care about the details of our lives, no matter how mundane. We become accustomed to the idea that there will always be eyes on us. Our parents cheer us on, caring much more about the game than the outcome. This feeling of being watched, this warm fetishization, this fame, cannot truly be appreciated until our audience dies and we are suddenly alone, competing in an empty stadium."*

Our fearless inquisitor has never been lost for words. And yet, here, he now finds himself wordless and adrift amongst a sea of sporting metaphors.

"I'm sorry," says the voice, *"We are experiencing a high frequency of calls, and I am afraid our time is up. I can transfer you to our Resolutions Department if that might be of further assistance moving forwards? But I have to tell you, our fees are upwards of £5,000 per hour from this point onwards."*

Resolutions Department? thinks our caller. *I think I've heard enough.*

1

You Got to Take These Dreams and Make Them Whole

Released on March 30, 1998, Pulp's sixth album, *This Is Hardcore,* may be as close to commercial suicide as you can get when recording an album in a burning studio with a noose around your neck. But its release also conveyed many other things, including an acknowledgement that drugs and fame are not all they're cracked up to be, and that pornography is a clear and pleasant danger for men with too much time on their hands. One thing it most definitely signified was the end of Britpop. *Good riddance to bad rubbish,* I hear you cry, but it's a truth barely acknowledged that only a band like Pulp, who'd formed almost twenty years previously – Jarvis Cocker formed the band at the City School in Sheffield in 1978 with schoolmate Peter 'Dolly' Dalton, who several years later became one of my closest friends whilst we were both attending Nottingham University – and spent the vast majority of those twenty years squandering in obscurity, could have successfully completed the task with so much style and vigour.

Of course, the jury is still out on how Britpop began in the first place, but it's interesting to note that Pulp had already spent the first fourteen years of their existence failing spectacularly before Warp Records imprint Gift released 'O.U. (Gone, Gone)' as a single, and the world barely took note. 'O.U.' may have been awarded Single of the Week by influential rock weekly *Melody Maker* – the same week as new-indie-kids-on-the-block Suede's debut single, 'The Drowners,' received the identical accolade – but this was surely just another false dawn. One year earlier, in 1991, the *New Musical Express* had heralded Pulp's latest flight of fancy, 'My Legendary Girlfriend' – the song that actually turned me on to Pulp in the first place – as 'fantastic, a throbbing ferment of night club soul and teen opera,' and then, as a matter of whimsy, Pulp themselves, as 'the greatest rock 'n' roll band in the world', but the band were still in the midst of a dispute with long-term adversaries, Fire Records, a label that had been sitting on their *Separations* album for three years, until that record finally appeared in 1992. It was all a bit *messy*.[1]

The year 1992 could be seen as Pulp's own *annus horribilis* – except, no doubt, that year must have been 1985, when, soon after signing to Fire, Cocker fell thirty feet off a window ledge whilst trying to impress a girl and ended up in hospital with a broken pelvis, wrist, and foot, temporarily requiring the use of a wheelchair – before eventually concluding that 1992 hardly changed anything at all really: a new set of life coordinates may have optimistically appeared on the horizon, but so did a counter-realisation that God had other plans. After Pulp signed to Island Records, several new singles, including 'Babies', 'Razzmatazz', 'Lipgloss', and 'Do You Remember the First Time', had started to trouble the Top 40, before their 1994 album *His 'n' Hers* hit the Top Ten. Then, one year later, *Different Class* went to number one, spawning four Top Ten singles, including 'Common People' and 'Mis-Shapes/Sorted For E's & Wizz', which both hit the number two spot, and 'Disco 2000' and 'Something Changed'.

By this time, all bets were off, except the success of *Different Class* – and 'Common People' in particular – hid a wider malaise. In June 1995, when Pulp stood in for the Stone Roses at Glastonbury, they may have blown the roof off the place, but they still looked and felt like outsiders. Three months later, on September 25, the band released their 'Sorted For E's & Wizz' single and the British tabloids had a field day, accusing the Sheffield five-piece of encouraging drug abuse, since the pre-release single had an inlay which, the *Daily Mirror* alleged, showed buyers how to make an origami coke wrap. The release coincided with the death of seventeen-year-old schoolboy, Daniel Ashton, who became the fifty-first person in Britain to die as a result of taking ecstasy. *The Mirror* ran a poll, their readers subsequently voting 2,112 to 770 that the record should be banned. Then, on February 19, 1996, when Cocker invaded the stage whilst Michael Jackson was performing 'Earth Song' at the Brit Awards, all hell broke loose.

That evening at Earls Court Exhibition Centre – and it's my contention that the night marked the Year Zero for what would one day become *This Is Hardcore* – Pulp had been nominated for four Brit Awards – Best Album, Best Group, Best Single, and Best Video – losing out to Oasis in the Album, Group, and Video categories, and to pop group Take That in the Single category. The band had also been booked that night to perform 'Sorted for E's & Wizz'. And on the same bill, making his first British TV appearance in twenty years, was Michael Jackson.

The Brits laid out the red carpet for the King of Pop, who was thirty-seven years old at the time, inventing the Artist of a Generation award so that he would agree to perform his recent Christmas number one hit, 'Earth Song', then allowing him to perform the song surrounded by groups of pre-pubescent girls and boys, just two years after he had settled out of court on a sexual abuse case brought against him by the father of thirteen-year-old Jordan Chandler. As a fellow broadcast performer, Jarvis was one of the few allowed to watch the run-through of Jackson's 'act' in rehearsals. 'I couldn't quite believe what I was seeing', he told *Smash Hits* magazine two months later. 'I found it extremely distasteful and crap'.[2]

Once Jackson started performing on the air that night, Jarvis became incensed. 'Something in me just snapped', he said. 'It really irked me that there were all these people with rags on, and him healing them all. He was obviously trying to exonerate himself from the child abuse allegations. Candida, our keyboard player, egged me on. I said, "Look, we could do something here, we're really near!" And she said, "Oh, you'd never do it."'

But Jarvis did do it, or more specifically, he leapt on stage, and waggled his arse to the crowd, making a strange kind of wafting gesture with his hands behind his back whilst doing so. It was pretty tame stuff when you think about it, and when Jarvis was ushered off stage by one of Jackson's henchmen, cleverly disguised as a dancer, he returned to his seat and thought nothing more of it. Well, apart from the fact that, according to Pulp drummer Nick Banks, all the audience were stamping and cheering: 'people kept coming up to him, slapping him on the back, giving him the thumbs-up and going, "Good move Jarvis!"'[3]

Much later, as Jarvis was trying to leave the venue, he was invited by a policeman and the Brits organisers to discuss the incident in his dressing room, whereupon he was arrested on suspicion of assaulting the children on the stage, which was news to him. 'I couldn't believe they were saying that at first', said Jarvis. 'Then, they carted me off to the police station, so it wasn't much of a joke.' Jarvis was questioned for two hours before being taken to Kensington Police Station, accompanied by comedian Bob Mortimer, who'd been in attendance at the Brits that night and offered to act as his legal counsel – Mortimer used to work in the legal department at Peckham Council – although he very nearly reneged on the offer when he realised Jackson had three heavyweight LA lawyers on his team. For his part, Mortimer remembers entering the room where Jarvis was being kept, enquiring what had happened, and receiving the reply, "I showed my bottom to Michael."

At three in the morning, after being informed that he would have to attend court to answer any charges laid against him on 11 March, Jarvis was released on bail. Later that day, he would make his way down to Brighton with the rest of Pulp to perform at Brighton Centre for the first night of the band's ten-date arena tour, a tour that would culminate with two shows at Wembley Arena on 1 and 2 March.

Michael Jackson decided to issue a statement. 'I'm sickened, saddened, shocked, upset, cheated and angry, but immensely proud that the cast remained professional and the show went on,' it said. Jackson's people also accused Jarvis of 'harming' three children. 'Jacko's Pulp Friction,' gasped the *Daily Express*. 'He's Off His Cocker,' screamed *The Sun*.

The *NME* started selling 'Jarvis is Innocent' T-shirts, and then, on Thursday, three days after the incident, they sent a writer to Pulp's show at Birmingham NEC Arena to canvass opinion of the public and Jarvis's bandmates. The *NME* ran a cover story with the headline, 'Wanna Be Startin' Something: Jarvis, Jacko and the True Story of the Brits.'

Jarvis released his own statement. 'My actions were a form of protest at the way Michael Jackson sees himself as some Christ-like figure with the power of healing', it said. 'The music industry allows him to indulge his fantasies because of his wealth and power. People go along with it even though they know it's a bit sick. I just couldn't go along with it any more. It was a spur-of-the-moment decision brought about by boredom and frustration. I just ran on the stage and showed off. I didn't make any physical contact with anyone as far as I recall. I certainly didn't push anybody off stage. I find it very insulting to be accused of attacking children. All I was trying to do was make a point and do something lots of other people would have done if only they'd dared.' The next day, a very charming, but slightly contrite Jarvis Cocker was interviewed by Chris Evans – Evans had actually presented the Brits earlier that week – on *TFI Friday*. Jarvis appeared live via a video link set up in the dressing room of the NYNEX Arena in Manchester, where Pulp was due to appear live later that evening. 'The police have got until March 11, which is when I've got to go back to the police station', he was keen to point out, 'and then, if they've thought of anything, then I'll get charged with it'.

By this point in proceedings, the tide had most definitely turned, with the cavalcade of approval for Jarvis's actions – there were even calls for him to be knighted – coinciding with the release of footage shot by David Bowie's camera crew – Bowie had received a Lifetime Achievement award at the Brits, presented to him on the night by (New) Labour leader Tony Blair – who'd filmed the whole evening, including Jackson's rendition of 'Earth Song' and Jarvis's stage invasion. The footage showed that Jarvis didn't knock any children off the stage, and all charges were dropped immediately. 'Among many other things I'm grateful to David Bowie for', said Jarvis, 'that was amazing'. Suddenly, even the *Daily Mirror*, who'd attacked the band for their origami wrap the previous year, came on board to back Jarvis, and by the following Thursday, they'd tracked the band down to Sheffield Arena – *oh, those intrepid reporters, what will they think of next?* – where they handed out free 'Justice For Jarvis' T-shirts.[4]

Many years later, in 2020, Cocker spoke to *The New York Times* about the events of that evening, admitting that it had 'changed my life forever' and affected him deeply. 'In the UK, suddenly I was crazily recognised and I couldn't go out anymore', he said. 'It tipped me into a level of celebrity I couldn't ever have known existed, and wasn't equipped for. It had a massive, generally detrimental effect on my mental health'. 'Maybe I was too acquiescent', Cocker reflected to *Time Out* when asked about his period as a tabloid mainstay. 'I just did everything that I was asked to do. This has been a fundamental change in my views. What I've realised is that the mainstream has an emasculating or castrating effect. You invent this thing, this shield with which you protect yourself against the world, and you lose control of it. Suddenly the tabloids, whose moral values I don't subscribe to, have an opinion on what you do'.[5]

More than two years after the Michael Jackson Incident – by which point longtime guitarist Russell Senior had jumped ship, claiming 'it wasn't creatively rewarding to be in Pulp anymore' – Pulp decided to end their affair with showbiz, and the movement they'd become associated with: Britpop.

The result was *This Is Hardcore*.

This Is Hardcore is Pulp's cry for help. The musical equivalent of Reggie Perrin's Grot shops – the album seemingly was designed to fail – the album is a sleazy run through porn and mental demise, whilst simultaneously chronicling Jarvis Cocker's disillusionment with his long-desired wish for fame, as expressed through the metaphor of pornography. Appropriately enough, it can also be seen as the final nail in Britpop's coffin, although you could be forgiven for thinking that all necessary factions of *The Big Four* had been here before: as far back as 1994, Suede had released *Dog Man Star* –'You could not find a less Britpop record', said Brett Anderson at the time, 'it's tortured, epic, extremely sexual and personal: none of these apply to Britpop' – in order to distance themselves from Britpop. Then, in February 1997, Blur (with *Blur*) went all Yank to do the same; and in August that year, Oasis released the bloated *Be Here Now*, an album containing only one track under four minutes in length. None of these Britpop-denying items of interest did much to spike that movement's allure, however, and it was left to Jarvis and Co. to reveal the truth: *the party's over and it's time to take stock.*

But this book is not about Britpop. Instead, it's about a giant, sprawling, flawed masterpiece of a record that manages to tackle some of the most inappropriately grown-up issues of the day: fame, ageing, mortality, drugs, and pornography. As part of the April 1998 *Select* magazine cover story, 'Death, Porn, Heroin – What's Eating Jarvis Cocker?', Jarvis told journalist Andrew Perry that *This Is Hardcore* is 'a bit about fame, actually, although its starting off point is porn'.[6] He continued:

> I could see some parallels there. I ended up watching a lot of porn on tour. If you get back to the hotel and you've got nothing to do, you put the adult channel on and have a look. It's the way that people get used up in it. You'd see the same people in films, and they'd seem to be quite alive, and then you'd see a film from a year later, and there's something gone in their eyes. You can see it, that they've done it all, and there's nowhere else to go. There seemed to be something really poignant about that to me. It seemed to be very similar to the way people get used up in the entertainment business. Obviously, television and everything thrives on these life stories of people. It doesn't matter whether it's a film star or a rock musician or anybody, it always seems to end tragically and you can't hide from the fact. You think, is that gonna happen to me as well then?

This Is Hardcore is music as confession therapy. The album had barely hit the shelves before *The Observer's* Lynn Barber hailed it as 'DIY therapy', which saw Cocker 'grappling with some horrendous problems – panic attacks, self-loathing, disgust and drugs', and Jarvis would go on to grapple with these themes again and again. And again.[7]

'There's something to do with realising an ambition that seems to curdle somebody's spirit in some way', Jarvis told

Select. 'So, it seemed appropriate to write about that. I was really relieved to write about it without referring to it directly, to have found some kind of image for it'. Then, in July 1998, he told *Time Out* magazine, 'Soft porn is just good-looking people being used to sell things. Hardcore porn takes that wrapping away, and reduces something that is actually quite emotional to a mechanical process. It's too much information. They pick angles that you wouldn't be able to see if you were making love to somebody. Things you shouldn't really see. So, it seemed a reasonable metaphor for success. You dream about what being a pop star will be like and, like most things, when you get it, it isn't how you imagined'.

As the *This Is Hardcore* promo campaign sauntered on – my PR company, Savage and Best, had been looking after the band since the early 1990s, and we must have set up almost fifty interviews to accompany the release of the album – Jarvis became ever more ebullient on the subject of all things *Hardcore.* 'Without wanting to sound trite', he told *Arena's* Paul Morley in May 1998, continuing:

> I would say that the basic message of *This Is Hardcore* is – be careful what you hanker after, it may come true and it won't be quite what you expected. And what the hard core is, it's the hard core of who you are, because in the end that's all you've got. And after everything that's happened to me, the life before fame, and then the fame, what's left of me, what carries on after the fun and games, is the hard core of who I actually am.[8]

That same month, in a bar in Toronto, he would tell Sean Plummer why they'd made such an unusual record:

We were in a different situation in that the last album had been successful. And, also, we'd been through quite a few changes personally. I'm not really a fan of self-analysis, but there are times in your life when you have to look at yourself and have a check on what it is that's driving you, what's motivating you to make a record. You've got to pay your mortgage off on your house - that's not a good reason to make music.[9]

In the 2003 film, *Live Forever*, Jarvis admits *This Is Hardcore* is dark:

I got the fear, because I got what I wanted I suppose, and the actual reality of that, I thought, were rubbish – and my way of dealing with that situation was just to get hammered as much as possible. *This Is Hardcore* was awful to write. It was definitely the worst period of my life. Taking drugs didn't help. You never hear people say, 'Oh, since he's been taking those drugs, he's become such a nice person.

By 2008, Jarvis was telling *The Guardian*'s Simon Hattenstone, 'I guess lots of people have one particular incident that overshadows just about everything else they've done in your life', and then, as if to confirm our suspicions, 'Although, I don't regret it as a moral action, the fact it will be the first line in my obituary is just a little disappointing. I'd like to think I'd given more to the world'.[10]

Naturally, he has, but it's interesting to note that as recently as July 2020, Jarvis was suggesting to the *Sunday Times* that the period leading up to the release of *This Is Hardcore* was 'a very strange time for me, because I'd achieved my lifetime's ambition, and then found that it didn't satisfy me'. And then, right on cue, he reiterates, 'Fame reminds me of pornography, of how pornography takes an amazing thing – love between two people expressed physically – and kind of grosses it out'. Finally, in September 2021, in the midst of an interview with Kate Mossman for the *New Statesman*, Jarvis finally admits what we've known all along: that crashing the Michael Jackson performance at the start of 1996 had had a toxic effect on him, and that, by the end of the year, he'd found himself in the middle of a 'nervous breakdown'.[11], [12]

2
Something Changed

By the end of March 1996, six weeks after the Michael Jackson Incident, *Melody Maker* was already suggesting that Jarvis Cocker was 'The Fifth Most Famous Man in Britain, behind John Major, Frank Bruno, Will Carling and Michael Barrymore'. A week earlier, *The Guardian*, in the midst of a two-page article analysing Pulp's success in the wake of Jarvis's Brit Award antics, had calculated that the band had earned three quarters of a million pounds worth of free advertising, and sold an extra 50,000 records as a result, whilst over at *The Sun*, a team of crack reporters had unearthed pictures of Jarvis's current wheels – a battered old Hillman Imp – wondering why a man of his stature and means should be driving around in such a decrepit old junkheap.[1]

Back at Pulp base camp, it was business as usual – of sorts. Although the band was still reeling from the unwelcome success of *Countdown 1992–1983*, a double compilation album released on 11 March featuring 'highlights' from the band's first three albums – *It*, *Freaks*, and *Separations* – together with non-album singles such as 'Dogs Are Everywhere' and 'Little Girl (With Blue Eyes)', and B-sides like 'Death Goes to the Disco'. The album reached No. 10 in the charts, becoming the only charting compilation of any Fire Records material, and was released by compilation specialists Nectar Masters. Jarvis – whose permission, along with that of the rest of the band, was not sought before release – put out a statement, urging anyone not to buy the album. 'Please', it said, 'I find it embarrassing to be honest. And also, the way it's packaged to look a bit modern, a bit like our sleeves now. It's a crap version, I wouldn't recommend it to anybody. And Fire Records never did us any favours when we were on the label. Being signed to that label was the single biggest thing that prevented us succeeding. It also made us split up'. However, matters were soon put right on 25 March, when 'Something Changed' – whose B-side, 'Mile End', had been included on the *Trainspotting* soundtrack a month earlier – was released as the fourth and final single from the band's breakthrough *Different Class* album, becoming the fourth consecutive Pulp single to crack the UK Top Ten. It would be the band's last release for more than eighteen months.

Two months later, Pulp set out on a thirteen date North American tour kicking off in Los Angeles on 21 May, running through to a show in Philadelphia on 9 June. The tour saw the band moving up to 800–1,200 capacity venues – no doubt, enhanced by a performance of 'Common People' on the David Letterman show in April – and selling out the 800-seater Toronto Opera House in three minutes and twenty seconds. By the time the band got to a sold-out 1,000-capacity show at New York's Irving Plaza, tickets were reselling at four times their street value. By this point, Jarvis's appearance in NYC had been heralded by *The New York Daily News* with the headline, 'Meet the Man Who Mooned Michael Jackson', whilst *Musician* magazine suggested that the episode had taken on 'a mythical quality'. You can see why Jarvis had been reticent about visiting the States in the first place – he'd originally considered wearing a bulletproof vest on stage, convinced he was going to get shot by insane Jacko fans – but apart from a few banners outside the David Letterman show, there was nothing to worry about. By the time *Select* magazine had caught up with Pulp in New York, he conceded, 'if, on my gravestone, they carved "Here Lies Jarvis Cocker – He Invaded Michael Jackson's Stage", then I would be very disappointed. I would consider that a bit of a failure'.[2]

Pulp's never-ending *Different Class* tour continued apace, with a twenty-two date run through Europe, starting off in Sweden a mere few days after they'd returned from the US. The *NME* followed them to Belgium, where Jarvis revealed that the music business lawyer who'd followed him into the dressing room at the Brits was 'so pissed he couldn't make sense'. You could be forgiven for thinking that everyone was still talking about *you know what* – I mentioned it once, but I think I got away with it – but at least by the time he left Belgium, Jarvis was moving onto new topics, announcing, 'Men get erections, you see. And people have so little direction in their lives, if your cock points in a certain direction, then you follow it, because at least it's a kind of imperative. You can't argue with a hard on, can you?' An early nod in the direction of *This Is Hardcore*, perhaps, but consider this: when Pulp returned to the UK after their Summer '96

American jaunt, they spent several days writing songs with no lyrics, since the words always come last, and Jarvis had no idea what he wanted to write about – yet. As *Melody Maker*'s Dave Simpson had noted some months earlier:

> Almost all his songs so far have been about the pre-fame Jarvis, the dreamer whose fantasies of love, lust and revenge lay unfulfilled. Now that they are fulfilled, what of Jarvis' muse? Will he continue to mine the same seam of his peculiar, solitary past? Or will he force himself to analyse his fame and focus on his success? And if so, can Jarvis' concerns post-fame be of as much interest as those from before? Can Jarvis Cocker keep sticking his pen right through the heart of the common people?

Pulp's last two concerts for fourteen months – okay, they played a private set for Holsten Pils in Barcelona (featuring a cover of Thin Lizzy's 'Whisky In The Jar') on 24 August – took place as headliners of the V Festival at Hylands Park in Chelmsford and Victoria Park in Warrington on 17 and 18 August 1996, events boasting a 70,000-strong contingent of fans, and performances from Super Furry Animals and Elastica, amongst others. However, the most significant appearance Pulp made around this period had taken place earlier that week, on 13 August, at the Clickimin Centre in the Shetland Islands – really just an excuse for Pulp keyboardist, Candida Doyle, to invite her relatives along to a gig, and for the band to go fishing whilst they were over there for a week – where the band performed a new song for the first time. The song was called, 'Help the Aged'.

In September 1996, Pulp were awarded the Mercury Music Prize for *Different Class*, after Island Records had held the release over for a year, despite the record being up against Oasis and Manic Street Preachers. To this day, the album remains the second most commercially successful Mercury Prize winner of all time (after Arctic Monkeys), having sold 1.5 million copies, but the band donated their £25,000 prize money to War Child, the music business charity helping children affected by the War in Bosnia. Two months later, they returned to the Townhouse Studios in Shepherds Bush – where they'd recorded *Different Class* – to record a new album, but events didn't go according to plan. In fact, the only song the band had – apart from 'Northern Souls', which was later overdubbed and released as 'Glory Days' on *This Is Hardcore* – was 'Help the Aged', which guitarist Russell Senior considered unworthy as a follow up to 'Common People'. 'So, I sabotaged it by playing blues guitar in the studio', he would say later.

At the time of the album's release, acclaimed *Hardcore* producer, Chris Thomas, who'd worked on *Different Class*, would tell *Mix* magazine:

> . . . in England they sold more than a million albums, which is really a lot there. Then, they went on the road for a year, and they found that difficult. And being under the looking glass was difficult for them, as it is for most people, and it made it difficult for Jarvis to write for the last album, and it went on for about eighteen months. In fact, Bryan Ferry was in the studio when we were starting out on this last Pulp record and he was telling me it had taken him

two years, and I said, 'I just cannot do that sort of thing'. Well, ha-ha-ha. The next thing I know the record I'm working on drags on for eighteen months![3]

Indeed, it did, but that delay was largely due to the fact that tensions in the band got so strained in that first October '96 session that recording was abandoned altogether after a few weeks – they wouldn't even rehearse again until February '97 – with just the one song barely completed.

Well, I say *one song*, but then there was the drama surrounding the track 'Cocaine Socialism'.

'I don't know if it was to do with exhaustion or nerves or what', Jarvis explained, as part of the sleeve notes for the 2006 Deluxe edition of *This Is Hardcore*, 'but when I came to sing "Cocaine Socialism" I just felt that something was awfully wrong. In all the years I'd been in the band I had never felt this way. I couldn't put my finger on it but it didn't feel right and I had to leave the studio right away and cancel the rest of the recording session. This was bad and I felt awful for letting the rest of the band down.'

Jarvis immediately took the opportunity to decamp to New York for three weeks, over Christmas and the New Year, checking in at the Paramount Hotel under a false name. Of the experience, he would later tell Andrew Perry in 1998:

I had a funny period where I went to New York on my own, which in retrospect wasn't the most sensible thing to do. But it was to get away from everything, and to have a think about what I wanted to do next, or even if I wanted to continue doing it anymore. I think I was just trying to get my head together, ready to go through this whole process. First of all, it's going to take you a certain amount of time to make the record, then it's going to take you quite a lot of time to go out and play to people. You're talking about two or three years out of your life. So, if you're going to go through that, you have to make sure that it's what you want to do, because if you go into it a bit half-heartedly, you're going to get really screwed up. So, I just wanted to go off to decide if it was what I wanted to do. But I probably could've done it in a less traumatic way.

Jarvis must have hidden the trauma well, since *Time Out*'s Garry Mulholland would subsequently inform him that composer/filmmaker Barry Adamson – who had collaborated with Jarvis around this time – told him that 'hanging around with you had given him some ambitions to be a pop star, because he admired the way you had fun with it'.

'Well, that's quite funny', laughed Jarvis, 'Because the last time I saw him was in New York at the end of 1996, when I was in a bit of a tangle and felt I had to go and sort me head out. I was not enjoying it at all, and wasn't sure what I was going to do. So, it's quite weird that he thought I was having a good time. If I hadn't had making a record to hold on to at that time. . . I don't know what kind of state I would've ended up in'.

Manhattan also provided another unwelcome distraction: one morning at 10 a.m., Tony Blair's campaign team managed to track Jarvis down at his hotel, asking if they could count on his support for the forthcoming election campaign. 'I told them to piss off', Jarvis said later, whilst also revealing that this wasn't the first time he'd been contacted and asked for his endorsement of New Labour. Of course, when Jarvis got back to Blighty, Tony Blair's over-exuberance was the least of his problems, as long-term guitarist and violinist Russell Senior handed in his notice.

Russell's departure had perhaps been on the cards for quite some time. In the Christmas 1996 edition of the *Pulp People* newsletter, Russell was asked what he considered to be his greatest regret, joshing innocently, 'Joining this group'. By 14 January 1997, however, he formally tendered his resignation. Russell had been in the band for thirteen years – born and raised in Sheffield, he'd originally reviewed a Pulp show in 1980 for his fanzine, and ended up joining the band some four years later in 1984 – so his departure appeared seismic, and when Radio 1 reported the news on 20 January, the band was forced to respond with a joint statement. 'Russell Senior has decided to leave Pulp after more than thirteen years, due to a desire to pursue new projects', it read. 'The split is entirely amicable and although the band are sad to see him go, they wish him all the best for the future. Pulp are currently rehearsing prior to recording their next album.' It's to Russell and the band's credit that they all sat around a table and hammered out a mutually agreeable settlement without a lawyer in sight.

Two years later, Russell would tell music site *musicOMH*, 'I was very proud of being in Pulp. I thought it was the best band in the world, when I was in it, but I want to be able to move on from it at some point.' Then, a year later, he told *Mojo*:

I'm proud of *Different Class*, but when we were doing it, I had a real sense we had lost it but just managed to hold it together for the album. On the tour, the atmosphere was very cold and I think we got complacent and ended up losing all connection with reality. The politics and hangers-on and also three members living in London. It just seemed hypocritical doing all these songs about Common People and not being like that – it had lost all connection with reality.

And then, in 2009, Russell would admit to *The Guardian*:

For years, we spent a lot of time in Transit vans. But suddenly it was all gold discs, condos, famous mates and people whose reality comes from cocaine, telling you you're great, night after night. I felt a revulsion for it. We were doing songs about Common People and it was, 'Jarvis, Prada's on the phone, they've got your outfit.' The last concert I did with Pulp was a corporate gig for a lager company in Barcelona. We were put up in a fantastic hotel, there were supermodels hanging around, but we were playing for bored executives. I felt myself backing away. We had become his backing band. Previously, the music always came collectively, from creative clashes, but I think Jarvis believed his own press and suddenly he was coming in with his own tunes.

When 'Help the Aged' was released as a single on 11 November 1997, there wasn't a Russell Senior writing credit in sight. And if that aborted recording session had told the remaining members of Pulp one thing, it was this: if they were going to get on with the recording of their most anticipated album to date, they'd have to do it the hard way.

3
This Is the Eye of the Storm

According to Pulp bassist Steve Mackey, Jarvis Cocker wrote all the lyrics to *Different Class* in two days. *This Is Hardcore* proved to be a much more difficult nut to crack. When the band finally met up for the first time, *sans* Russell, at their rehearsal room in Farringdon in early 1997, the mood had been lifted. Russell's departure, rather like Bernard Butler's departure from Suede in July 1994, meant that everyone in the room wanted to be there. Pulp was a gang again.

The only problem: after a period of self-doubt, and another period of self-reflection in New York, Jarvis appeared to be suffering from writer's block, an affliction that was acknowledged by other members of the band at the time.

'The lyrics always seem to be the very, very last thing that ever get done', drummer Nick Banks told *The Face* magazine in October 1997, 'so you never know what the lyrics are going to be. The group never meddled in the words. There's never been any need. It's always been: "Here are the words." And we've always gone: "Great!" But it's become quite obvious that he's been finding it more difficult to come up with a real angle on life and what people are actually thinking and how life actually goes on.'[1]

Correspondingly, Jarvis has suggested that any lack of inspiration on his part did not last very long. 'I probably revised the words on this one more,' he told the *NME*'s Stephen Dalton, a week before the album's release, 'but there was never a point where I couldn't write anything. So, it wasn't writer's block, just mild constipation.'[2]

In late 1996, Jarvis moved house from London's Ladbroke Grove neighbourhood, where he'd lived and written Pulp songs since 1993, to Maida Vale, where, he told the *NME*'s Roger Morton in late 1997, 'people don't want to demean themselves by acknowledging you'. It's been suggested that the move coincided with Jarvis's period of self-reflection, or a slowdown in his lyrical output at any rate. Guitarist Mark Webber offers a different perspective, suggesting that the lyrics he wrote towards the end of the year, on songs like 'Sylvia', were more in line with *Different Class*, whereas the ones he wrote in early 1997, like 'The Fear' and 'This Is Hardcore', were bleak and death-obsessed.[3]

Whilst we're on the subject of Mark Webber, I should probably explain his newly-acquired status as Pulp's lead guitarist. Mark accounted for his presence in the band whilst speaking to *Q* magazine in March 1996:

'When I was fifteen and a half, I decided that I wanted to write a fanzine,' he said. 'I lived in Chesterfield. Pulp played at the Arts Centre and I interviewed them. They were totally weird. Jarvis had just had his accident and he came onstage in a Victorian wheelchair. He performed all the way through, then at the end he stood up and walked off. I got to know them and over the years I helped out with the light show, ran the fan-club and became the tour manager. From 1992 I was playing second guitar on stage, and on *Different Class* I got involved in song-writing. Last summer they had a big meeting. They gave me this once-in-a-lifetime offer. I was flattered and shocked. They didn't have to do it.'[4]

Some eighteen months later, Mark seemed a natural choice to step up from rhythm guitarist to lead. Mark counts minimalist composer La Monte Young as one of his heroes, and it's probably true to say that some of the band's modernistic guitar atmospherics generate from his side of the tracks.

Having said that, it's just as important to note that *This Is Hardcore* also marks the point at which bassist and programmer Steve Mackey came to the fore.

'I feel I can talk about this album because I've been very involved in it', Steve told *Select* magazine in April '98. 'Politics of bands are something you can't explain to anyone, but, unfortunately, bands aren't democratic. If they were, it wouldn't lead to anything. There's a point where someone has to take the lead. When we started it, I was in quite a state for the first few months. Since we finished touring, I spent nearly all my time concentrating on using technology. There's still a lot of people who are very old-fashioned, even in our band – it's like using something from someone else's song is somehow not how it should be done. Mark despises my musical taste.

Anything involving beats – Mo' Wax, Aphex Twin and that kind of stuff – he just can't cope with it. Two or three songs started from the sampling process.'

Drummer Nick Banks spoke about those early *Hardcore* sessions in Mark Sturdy's book, *Truth and Beauty: The Story Of Pulp*:

'After Russell wasn't with us, it did free something up a little bit. Certainly, Mark felt easier to be able to input more. There was more space in the room, and we'd lost that bit of tension. We started to use samplers as well at this point – Steve was really getting into that and using computers and stuff, so we had "This Is Hardcore", with the sample on it, the horns taken off Peter Thomas', – more of this, later – 'and I'd got an electronic drum set from Yamaha to play with that gave us "Seductive Barry"; the drone at the start came from my electronic drum.'[5]

Those early *Hardcore* album demos, recorded in January and February '97 at Fortress Studios, included 'Can I Have My Balls Back Please?' – which was actually the first song written after Jarvis came back from the US – 'Street Operator', 'Modern Marriage', 'You Are the One', and 'My Erection', which didn't make the official recording sessions – instead ending up on the *This Is Hardcore* deluxe edition bonus disc released in 2006 – and 'I'm a Man', 'The Fear', 'We Are the Boyz', 'TV Movie', 'Party Hard', and 'Sex Symbols' – an early working title for 'Seductive Barry' – which did. Another song, 'Grown Ups', remains unreleased in any form, never progressing beyond its instrumental phase. But was the brutal axing of some songs rather than others indicative of a wider brief: to pursue a low-key sound at the expense of chart success? Keyboardist Candida Doyle seems to think so. 'We probably could have done another *Different Class*', she told the *NME* in March 1998, 'but Jarvis didn't want to. There were songs that could have been instant hits, but we took them off'.

Pulp started work on *This Is Hardcore* in earnest, at the Townhouse Studios in March 1997, but by April, they'd already become distracted by the prospect of recording the theme for the forthcoming James Bond flick, *Tomorrow Never Dies*. The opportunity had actually been part of an open call for submissions, but the band's efforts weren't selected – Marc Almond, Swan Lee, and Saint Etienne also submitted tracks before the studio opted for Sheryl Crow's 'Tomorrow Never Dies' as the film's theme. The track instead ended up as the B-side – reworked and retitled 'Tomorrow Never Lies' – for the 'Help the Aged' single released at the end of the year, while the earlier version of the song – 'Tomorrow Never Dies!' – eventually surfaced on the Deluxe edition of *This Is Hardcore*.

It's nigh-on-impossible to ascertain which songs were recorded in which order during the Townhouse and Olympic Studios *Hardcore* sessions, although, when several work-in-progress cassettes were auctioned off by music memorabilia auction house Omega Auctions in early 2021, the sale shed some light on the matter. But what about, 'It's a Dirty World', a song quite definitely recorded during this period? 'Towards the end of the album sessions', Jarvis explains in the sleeve notes for the 2006 special edition of *This Is Hardcore*, 'we came up with this song which ended up being left off the final album. It was based on a girl I'd met in a nightclub who called herself "Miss High-Kick" (with good reason). I never had any kind of thing with her but she. . . caught my imagination. The insistent "beep" noise that goes through the track is the electronic horn I had on my bike at the time. God knows who played the timbales'. The song would also end up on the 2006 bonus disc of *This Is Hardcore*.

So they were quite busy then, you might be thinking, and you'd be right. Pulp even found time to go into another studio for a B-sides session – produced by the band themselves – to record 'The Professional' and the dub-techno-driven, vocoder-laden 'Ladies Man', which would both end up as B-sides for the 'This Is Hardcore' single, and 'That Boy's Evil', which surfaced on the flipside of the 'A Little Soul' single released in June 1998. Then, in October 1997, Pulp would appear on David Arnold's James Bond tribute album, *Shaken and Stirred*, performing Rita Coolidge's 'All Time High'.

After playing over fifty shows the year before as part of their Different Class tour, Pulp made only one live appearance in 1997, playing the Barbican Hall in London on 31 October. The concert, a benefit for La Monte Young and his partner Marian Zazeela, who'd been ill for quite some time, featured appearances by Nick Cave and Warren Ellis, Spiritualized, Gavin Bryars, and the English Chamber Orchestra. It was a strange night, but what did one expect from an event that disclaimed right on the tickets, 'The Purpose of This Concert Is Not Entertainment'. Oh, and there was no mention of Pulp on the tickets, either – Savage and Best were under instructions to inform potential reviewers, 'This is not a Pulp gig' – which is why erstwhile Pulp-ite Anthony Genn helped out on guitar, and Pulp only played a twenty-minute set, featuring three brand new songs: 'Seductive Barry' – which was then known as 'Love Scenes' – featuring the English Chamber Orchestra, 'This Is Hardcore', featuring Gavin Bryars on piano and the ECO again, and 'Help the Aged'. It was not a Pulp gig, but somehow it felt just perfect.

As 1997 cantered towards its inevitable conclusion, Pulp busied themselves by taking over John Peel's Radio 1 show for three consecutive evenings in November – which primarily involved Jarvis and Steve playing records by Sheffield acts such as I'm So Hollow and Artery, and new acts like Tiger and Add N to X – to coincide with the release of Pulp's nineteenth single.

The song chosen to advertise the wares of *This Is Hardcore*, an album not due to be released for another four months, was 'Help the Aged', and though the single may have hit the Top Ten, it was a *blink-and-you-missed-it* affair. In light of its lacklustre commercial success, the vultures began to circle, with the *NME* saying at the time of its release, that 'Help the Aged' made 'as much commercial sense as making your first live foray for eighteen months at a live charity event for an obscure avant-garde American composer at the Barbican'. It also might explain why Island Records scrapped the original November release date for *This Is Hardcore*, and sent it scuttling back into next March – and why Pulp didn't stop fiddling with the album until January.

4
That Goes in There

I'm not having a go, I'm just saying.

The first thing that hits you round the face is the artwork. When I first encountered it, I wasn't sure if it felt quite right looking at it, let alone touching it, feeling it, handling it, *thinking* about it. Believe it or not, I even had a hard time thinking that it really existed. But there it was, Pulp, lovely Pulp, my Pulp, your Pulp, *our* Pulp, had decided to illustrate their latest record with a cover featuring a picture of a naked woman crouched and draped – flung? – across a puce leather sofa, her elongated neck arcing unsettlingly towards her open mouth and detached eyes, the album's hot pink title stamped obscenely across her skin. On closer inspection, one couldn't actually tell whether the woman was alive or dead. Or was she indeed not real, and actually a blow-up doll? And was she even, perhaps recovering from, or in the midst of, a degrading sexual act?

Before I had a decent chance to consider my innermost feelings on the subject, I got a call from a radio station, asking whether I could come into their news studios to defend the use of such a provocative image as part of such a prominent band's album artwork. Posters for the album on the London

Underground system had just been defaced with graffiti stating 'This Offends Women', 'This Is Sexist', and 'This Is Demeaning', and I wasn't entirely sure I disagreed with any of the protestors who'd voiced their concerns in such a timely fashion. *The Independent on Sunday* took a typically meta stance on the subject, suggesting that 'whoever designed the controversial poster must be feeling pretty pleased with themselves: it has gained the pop group plenty of extra publicity'. *Not everything's about publicity, you know,* I must have thought at the time, somewhat disingenuously, although, rather worryingly, the paper went on to suggest that 'the woman looks as if she had been raped'. Either way, it turned out Mrs. Muggins here had to get up at 6 a.m. one morning to face a cross-examination from some of the angriest people in the country.

You could say I was out of my depth, or you could say I hadn't prepared properly. Either way, my innocent musings on the subject of porn as art as marketing as promotion, were repeated in the news bulletin on the hour, every hour, for as long as it took for my friends to start ringing me, to ask if that really was me on the radio sounding so harangued and upset. And was I actually, alright? At one point, I think I may have read out a statement which said, 'Anyone who listened to the album and thought that Pulp are in any way sexist is a fool', which I am sure kicked the discussion into the long grass for several minutes, but when the album artwork's designer, Peter Saville, claimed that 'our first proposals for posters on the Tube and on the backs of buses were rejected, which is a triumph really', I winced at the prospect. 'For the whole thing just to have passed without a murmur would have been a great disappointment', continued Saville. 'To have to redo things is slightly rewarding.'[1]

It was art director and graphic designer Saville – best known for his album sleeve designs for Factory Records, a label he co-founded alongside Tony Wilson and Alan Erasmus in 1978 – that Jarvis and Steve had originally commandeered – via an initial phone call, and then a visit to Peter's swanky, two-thousand-square-foot Mayfair apartment – to 'present Pulp more as a rock band', according to Saville, since 'the music was a lot deeper, darker and moodier'. Saville himself understood the title to be more about the 1997 spirit of Pulp, rather than pornography. 'It was the new, hard, resolute spirit in Pulp', he told author and *New Statesman* design critic Hugh Aldersey-Williams in May 1998. 'The band wanted to be taken seriously. Jarvis talked to us about fame and how it changes the world around you – yet you are still supposed to be the same person'. In 2023, Saville wrote an essay entitled, 'The Apartment' for Paul Burgess and Louise Colbourne's 2023 photobook *Hardcore: The Cinematic World of Pulp* – a lush visual celebration of *This Is Hardcore*, featuring unseen photography, behind-the-scenes interviews and revealing visuals – in which he revealed that:

> When working on the campaign material for the album, when it came to ads on the side of double decker buses, Transport for London were prepared to accept the album image alone on a bus, and they were prepared to accept solely the title *This Is Hardcore* – but they were not prepared to accept the image and the title together![2]

As a source of visual inspiration, the young American painter John Currin proved to be the key to the project. Currin's work, as described by Aldersey-Williams, 'typically portrays seedy, ageing playboys and improbably fulsome women in a hyper-realistic style.' Much later, whilst writing in *The Guardian* in 2003 – under the banner headline, 'They're not grotesque – they're beautiful' – Jarvis said that he was 'struck by Currin's images of powerful men', continuing:

> They are surrounded by women who seem to be sucking up to them, but really, they're thinking: 'What a jerk!' They're always old blokes with beards, and young women; that resonated at the time. I especially recognised his Martini Man advert paintings – the works he did using adverts from *Penthouse* and other magazines. He would take these photos of men in swimming pools, surrounding bikini-clad women looking up admiringly, but then paint over them so that the women were grimacing.[3]

Pulp would go on to use Currin's painting, 'The Neverending Story', as part of the artwork for the 'Help the Aged' single, and he seemed a natural fit for a record sleeve that was likely to cause as much fuss as the rest of Currin's work to date. Having said that, the cover turned out to be quite unusual for Currin, since he's a painter and the images he ended up producing are photographs.

Jarvis goes on to explain how Saville got Currin to come up with scenarios for the sleeve:

> The pictures were shot in London's Hilton Hotel – by fashion photographer Horst Diekgerdes – which is

supposed to be a luxury place, but in fact it's a bit tacky. His pictures showed people in luxurious settings not really fitting in properly – which at the time really fitted in with what the band was talking about. Without being too literal about it, he communicated the general discomfort that was being felt by Pulp.

For his part, Saville's essay reveals that 'John .. and I soon established a fluency between ourselves, identifying references, specifically material of an "adult nature", which we'd share in order to define the type of image we wanted to achieve.'

'There is a shared aesthetic between John's paintings and the characters in Jarvis's songs', Currin's art dealer, Sadie Coles, would explain to Dylan Jones in a *Sunday Times* article at the time. 'Essentially, they are both dealing with human frailty, and faded glamour. Cocker seems genuinely excited by the possibilities and the power of visual art, but although he's undoubtedly a great chronicler of our times, and there is often a genuine poetic quality to his writing, he's got quite a sad demeanour.'[4]

Once the photographs had been chosen – some of them feature band members gazing somewhat forlornly at semi-naked women in semi-provocative, though perhaps ambivalent, poses, whilst the centre spread is an uber-glossy pic of a heavily made-up Jarvis sitting at the hotel bar alongside actor slash model John Huntley – Saville's long-term accomplice, Howard Wakefield, digitally manipulated them. Paul Hetherington was also heavily involved in the design process, using a particular effect on all the photographs

– an Adobe Photoshop filter called Smart Blur. 'It gave the photographs a very painterly quality', says Wakefield, although Saville is quick to point out, 'we don't quite know what it – *Smart Blur* – does. But fascinating things happen between A and B that are not aesthetics-based'. Correspondingly, Aldersey-Williams would suggest, 'at full strength, it alters an image so that it looks as if it was painted by numbers. But used gently, it nudges it from photographic reality into painterly photorealism'.

Of course, all this kerfuffle fails to address the fact that when Diekgerdes shot Pulp at the Hilton Hotel in Park Lane – as part of a tableau of larger-than-life characters, and in order to create 'a weird world' – the band subsequently saw the photographs, and decided that they wanted something more *hardcore* for the cover itself. An image of Steve Mackey and a male actor standing facing each other was subsequently rejected by both Jarvis and Steve as being too weak. By now, everyone had run out of money, but a final dash to Saville's apartment – which he'd turned into a swanky celebration of a 1970s 'shag pad' with the help of Hacienda designer Ben Kelly – for a photo shoot proved successful, resulting in the actual front cover shot.

Addressing the not-quite-real appearance of the model, Aldersey-Williams explains in his piece for the *New Statesman*, 'Rather than paint Cocker and his confreres, Currin art-directed scenarios in which the members of the band appeared alongside anonymous models, models chosen for their super-real characteristics – the too amazing body, the too-perfect skin. They look perfect, yet there's something that tells you they are not.' Strangely enough, this was *exactly* what the band were looking for – an image that accurately represented the themes in the music – but does it work? And should it have been allowed to work?

Of course, in a nutshell, my main issue with the *This Is Hardcore* artwork is that *it's not really a painting, is it?* Instead, for all intents and purposes, several men have ensured that the camera has interceded between you and the subject, and we've just gone straight back to pornography, and talking about pornography, all over again. Which, presumably, is what Pulp wanted in the first place. Jarvis Cocker would go on to explain that 'one of the themes of the album was the deadening and dehumanising nature of pornography', but does that really excuse the image from any offence it might cause? To which the reply might be: *so what image are Pulp supposed to use to illustrate their music?* Which, I would counter with: *I'm sorry, but a snuff movie pretending not to be a snuff movie is still a snuff movie.*

But consider, if you will, the furore that surrounded Vladimir Nabokov's novel *Lolita* upon its release. Now, I am not naïve enough to suggest that this 'fuss' remotely resembled that surrounding the release of *This Is Hardcore*, but there are some similarities nonetheless – not least the fact that younger generations now draw attention to acts of sexual harassment and victimisation in a way that older generations wouldn't have bothered passing comment on.

Originally published by Paris Olympia Press in 1955, *Lolita* was rescued from obscurity – and the porn shops of Paris – by the author Graham Greene, after he named it as one of the three best books of the year in the 1955 Christmas issue of the *Sunday Times*. As a collector of rare books, I have always been fascinated by the book's publishing history – an original Paris edition of the book, signed and dedicated to Greene from Nabokov himself, was briefly owned by Bernie Taupin, and ended up selling for $264,000 at Christie's auction house in 2002 – but it is the book's reviewing history that I find most intriguing. Back when Greene was lauding the book, the *Sunday Express* called it 'sheer unrestrained pornography' and its editor, John Gordon, 'the filthiest book I have ever read'. Upon its first publication in the US several years later, in August 1958 to be exact, *The New York Times* called it 'repulsive, highbrow pornography', which, when you think about it, is not a million miles away from the point our Underground protesters were trying to make in the first place. As part of an excellent piece in *Vice* magazine, headlined 'This Bullshit World Was Predicted by Pulp's This Is Hardcore', Andrea Domanick suggested it was 'hard to say whether the subway vandals missed Pulp's point, or helped make it', but you could still imagine a world where Pulp, Peter Saville, Horst Diekgerdes, Howard Wakefield, Paul Hetherington, and John Currin all joined up with the vandals for a sit-in against the artwork, protesting both for and against its beautiful-not-grotesque profanities.[5]

By 1998, the year *This Is Hardcore* hit record stores, the Board of the Modern Library had already set about voting *Lolita* No. 4 on its list of the twentieth century's greatest English-language novels, where it has remained ever since. In the decades following its publication, the book has reached almost canonical standing amongst scholars – by 2015, *The New Yorker* was arguing that '*Lolita* secured for Nabokov over time a reputation as a master of English prose second only to Joyce' – but it is constantly being re-evaluated as a piece of work that perpetuates a toxic sexualization of young girls.[6]

And herein lies the rub: for just as the model for the *This Is Hardcore* shoot couldn't speak for herself – although, the eighteen-year-old Belarusian 'up-and-coming glamour model' Ksenia Zlobina did tell *FHM* magazine that 'the shoot was fun. Jarvis is very nice, very shy' – so Lolita is silenced by the novel's narrator, Humbert Humbert. As a result, we end up objectifying both Ksenia and Lolita, since we know so little about them. Nabokov famously declared that he 'didn't give a damn for public morals', but he also described Humbert Humbert as 'a vain and cruel wretch who manages to appear "touching"', so I think he knew what he was doing. As do we.[7]

On that note, I have to take issue with the way the woman is positioned. And the fact that when Peter Saville decided to use 'a censorship-type approach to the typography, as if it had been stamped by the Board of Censors', the title is carefully positioned between the eyebrow, chin and arm, and it just makes me think it's stamped on her face like she's owned. And that's with the proviso that I have some sympathy with Jarvis when he told *Melody Maker* in June 1998 that 'the idea behind the picture was that, initially, it would be attractive, you'd look at the picture and realise it's a semi-clad woman. But then her look is vacant. It almost looks as if she could be dead, or a dummy. So, it was supposed to be something that would draw you in and then kind of repel you a bit. That was on purpose'. As much as I agree with Jarvis that the works of John Currin are beautiful, and not grotesque, I guess I can't help feeling conflicted by that cover.[8]

Perhaps, in the spirit of fairness and compromise, I should leave the last word to Aldersey-Williams. 'Once Saville had massaged the pictures with his computer', he notes, 'the result is a layer cake of reality and artifice: real model, looks unreal; camera never lies, but the computer embellishes the truth. This is why, even on close examination – especially on close examination – it is impossible to decide about the woman on the album cover'.

So, there you have it.

And anyway, I'm not having a go. I'm just saying.

5
The Sound of Someone Losing the Plot

I've just stepped out of the Underground. I'm slightly out of breath, and my heart is beating wildly. I think this is Oxford Circus, but it's difficult to tell: I got on the tube at Highgate but had to change trains at Euston, as there was some kind of altercation on the station platform involving some angry people who'd been defacing posters and throwing them onto the track. I saw one of them being led away by a policeman. She looked very angry indeed.

I look around, catch sight of Top Shop, and breathe a sigh of relief. Never have I been more excited to see such an identifiably British women's clothing landmark in my life. And there, in the distance, right at the end of the street, is another landmark: Centre Point. I'm on the right track.

I head off in the direction of Centre Point, crossing the road before I get to Marks and Spencer. And there it is, my destination. HMV. The shop has been standing on the same spot for what seems like an eternity, and I don't know what I would do if it closed down, let alone one day be replaced by an American candy store, perhaps one of fifteen between Oxford Circus and Marble Arch.

Having said that, I am not really used to big record shops. They're like department stores, where everyone who works there doesn't really know anything about what they're selling. 'I may as well have asked a monkey', my dad would have said when a shop assistant had pointed him in entirely the wrong direction to try to find a jumper or a suit. He always hated shopping anyway, but it would have been nice to have spent just one day without an altercation of some kind. 'And how old was that person anyway? Twelve?'

The young boy behind the counter today is not twelve, but perhaps not much older.

"Good morning, Madam," he says, when I walk towards him purposefully. "How can I help you today?"

Madam, I say to myself silently. *How old does he think I am?* I shake my head gently. I'll have him know, I only turned thirty a few years back. In fact, I am the same age as that singer from Pulp, you know, the gangly one with the glasses, the one who manages to look both smart and scruffy at exactly the same time. And he's not old. He might look old, but he's not *actually* old.

"I hope so," I reply to the young boy, barely into his teens. "I bought this album in here the other day, and it appears to have the wrong record inside." I open the plastic HMV bag, and take out its contents. "It's Pulp's new album," I say, "*This Is Hardcore.*" Somewhat embarrassed, I hand the record over to the shop assistant. He looks at the cover suspiciously. "Sorry, about the cover," I say, "I think it's meant to be like that. I read somewhere that it's supposed to be something that draws you in and then kind of repels you a bit." I resist the temptation to add, "that's on purpose, that is."

The boy looks at me suspiciously, as if he can see through me and has worked out that I have been carefully selected by his boss and sent to his department to test his patience in circumstances such as these. He had one of those in last month, a woman complaining that the Madonna album she'd just bought, *Ray of Light*, was 'too grown up' for her daughter. *Where were her fun songs like 'Material Girl' and 'Holiday' and what was she supposed to do with this electric rubbish?* The boy had really wanted to correct the woman by saying "don't you mean, *electronica* rubbish?" but he thought he'd get into trouble with his boss, so he didn't say anything. Instead, he wondered how the woman could have spent the best part of fifteen years bypassing the golden years of Madonna's development as an artist, through songs like 'Like a Prayer' and 'Vogue', until she ended up in the ambient, trip-hop, and, yes, *electronica hell* of *Ray of Light*. And why couldn't there be more customers like the ones who'd appeared to be so happy and content when they were buying Mariah Carey and Celine Dion records the other day? You never got any trouble with those people.

The boy sighs, deciding he will have to deal with me.

"Pulp?" he says quizzically. "I've heard of them. Aren't they the ones who did 'Common People' a couple of years ago? Didn't their singer attack Michael Jackson on stage a while back?"

"No," I reply in exasperation. "I mean, yes, they are responsible for 'Common People,' but no, he didn't attack anyone. It's a long story," I add, almost apologetically. "Anyway, something's wrong, I don't think you put the right record in."

Carefully, gingerly, the young boy takes the inner sleeve out of its much bulkier jacket, before expertly removing one of the vinyl records within.

"Looks good, so far," he points out. "The label says Pulp and This Is Hardcore." He points to the round piece of paper in the centre of the record. "Look, it even says the name of the record label – Island Records."

"I know what it says," I say, matter-of-factly. "But something's wrong."

The boy sighs again, takes two paces over to the record player, situated handily at the far end of the counter, and places the record on the turntable. He presses a button, and the needle makes its agonizingly slow journey towards the record.

The music starts up and, suddenly, the store is transformed into the set of a horror movie, some violins and an EBow guitar playing consecutive, repetitive high notes, then low notes, and a suitably treated bass guitar, all competing with each other as part of a movie soundtrack, heralding the arrival of a dark, twisted brute of a song, lumbering into view. It sounds like nothing on earth. It certainly doesn't sound like Pulp.

'This is our 'Music from a Bachelor's Den, the sound of loneliness turned up to ten, a horror soundtrack from a stagnant waterbed, and it sounds just like this', sings the man in a scary voice, sounding like he's contacting us from beyond the grave – or, perhaps, from a retirement home for bewildered rock stars. I've already remembered that *Music for a Bachelor's Den* was a series of lounge music compilations released in the early 1990s, before the voice continues with, 'This is the sound of someone losing the plot, making out they're happy when they are not', and I realise I am in the middle of some raw psychological drama where the singer, seemingly paranoid from excessive drug use, is confessing to all sorts of sins. The song, which I notice from the record sleeve is called 'The Fear', effortlessly segues from the warped buzzsaw instrumentation of the verse into a chorus of damaged angels, harmonizing delicately, *menacingly*. Is this what bassist Steve Mackey was referring to when he said he'd been keen to 'modernise the Pulp sound' whilst sequencing the album alone with producer Chris Thomas at a studio in Shepherd's Bush?

"He doesn't sound very happy, does he?" says the boy behind the counter. "Is it all like this?"

"I don't know," I say. "I was worried about playing the whole record and damaging it, and not being able to change it for the right record, so I stopped playing it after a while – just in case."

The boy nods, as if in agreement.

And then, a funny thing happens. I suddenly start to remember some of the reviews of the record I have read in the last few days. '"The Fear" sounds like a mock-gothic Hammer House of Horror theme tune', noted *New Musical Express*. 'It's the sound of fingernails scraping down a blackboard heart, the panic-stricken screech of brakes this far from that pram, the awful, sobbing howl you hear downstairs when the phone rings too late to be social', moaned *Melody Maker*. *Select* magazine screamed:

> This is a record dealing with breakdown, it has none of rock's traditional dramatic glorification of mental and physical collapse. Instead, the ennui, the meaninglessness, the endless melancholy is primped up with a dash of

greasepaint, a swelling show-stopping chorus and the sense that, even now, the show must go on. It's all there in opener, 'The Fear.'

And then I remember an interview Jarvis had given to *The Guardian* three days before the record came out:

'The way to get through the things that were frightening me was to actually write a song about it', Jarvis told Caroline Sullivan. '"The Fear" was about panic attacks. Certain decades have certain illnesses, like with the eighties it was ME, and in the nineties it's panic attacks. I wasn't happy at the time I wrote it, and I was thinking more than I ought to about whether it was worth doing another album at all because I felt like *Different Class* had said it all. It frightened me, to think that might be it. I find it funny, that song, because it's so over the top – your sex life is gone, there's not just a monkey on your back but it's built a house there. It's funny because it's so extreme.'[1]

"I'm sorry," I say to the boy behind the counter. "I think I've made a terrible mistake. Can I have my Pulp record back please?"

*

The pay off line for all the fun and nonsense outlined above, arrives in the form of a very odd little couplet that Jarvis employs, almost as an aside, when he gently hollers, 'You're gonna like it, but not a lot'. Naturally, if anyone can holler gently, it's Jarvis Cocker, but you know the in-joke is entirely meant for us Brits. Indeed, once one has finished sniggering fondly at the reference to the catchphrase utilized by the erstwhile omnipresence of the now-deceased magician-turned-gameshow-host Paul Daniels, one is left to ponder how Jarvis gets away with such frivolities at all. But that's the point, writer Nick Hornby suggests in the midst of his review of Pulp's 'very wonderful' new album in *Spin* magazine, since it's a lyric that 'goes some way toward explaining Pulp's appeal in the UK. For a start, it's resolutely English. . . and you wouldn't catch any other pop musician in the entire history of the world even conceding, privately, that Paul Daniels exists. Cocker, however, lives in the same world as the rest of us, and admits as much without sounding too mundane or blowing his chic.'[2]

The scariest thing to note about 'The Fear' is not that it doesn't just sound like the end of Britpop, it actually sounds like the end of the world. It may be an ode to coked-up paranoia, a clarion call to the lonely and disenfranchised. '"The Fear" is about a lot of people who have suffered from the hedonism of the past four or five years', Jarvis told *Deluxe* magazine in July 1998. 'Some of them ended up in mental health day centres. I know that 'cause two of my flatmates work in them.'[3] But the song is almost overwhelmingly bleak at times. One listen and you're immediately transported to a psychodrama that's genuinely unsettling. *Where's my loveable Jarvis gone?* one could be forgiven for thinking. And then, once the song has really gotten going, we get some gorgeously menacing, John Barry-tinged string arrangements – Nicholas Dodd was responsible for orchestration – and you can almost hear Barry's TV theme song to *The Persuaders* popping its head above the parapet, as if to confirm we're not likely to get out of the woods without a fright. And then, when Jarvis nonchalantly leads us back into the belly of the beast, he delivers the line, 'And the chorus goes like this', with such petrified grace, that you don't know where to look. It's postmodernism writ large, six simple words that Morrissey would kill for. Nick Hornby actually goes on to suggest that *This Is Hardcore* made it clear that Pulp had outgrown Britpop, and Cocker belonged 'up there with Ray Davies and Costello and Morrissey, those who look at England with a satirist's eye and a balladeer's heart'. It's a lyric that sugar-coats the message we've got coming up – *we're washed up, we're finished, we've got nothing left to give.*

The song continues apace with, 'A monkey's built a house on your back, you can't get anyone to come in the sack, and here comes another panic attack', and you know that, at its most corrosive, 'The Fear' is Jarvis Cocker holding a mirror up to himself, so we can see ourselves. And whilst all this is going on – I mean, during the song's so-called chorus – there's a screeching choir featuring Mandy Bell, Carol Kenyon and Jackie Rawe, and you just know what's coming next. 'So now you know the words to our song, pretty soon you'll all be singing along', sings Jarvis, all-meta, and it's like we know they know we had it coming, and they know we know they know we had it coming.

And that self-analysis thing bears further fruit when you consider Jarvis's comments at the time:

"The liberating thing for me in 'The Fear' was to really go over the top and lay it on very thick with all these bad things," he said, "On a personal level 'The Fear' actually helped me by looking at the stuff and confronting it and saying 'yeah, it's bad.' Once you've used it and made it into a song, then it wasn't scary anymore for me."

Inadvertently, we seem to have stumbled across a private session between Cocker and his therapists. And for the purposes of our discussion, we, the listeners, are his therapists.

"Sometimes, there's too much to take in," he adds, "and it seems as though the mind shuts off and just feeds back on itself, and you get in a panic, convinced you're going to die. Putting yourself under this kind of pressure makes it worse. So instead of 'avert your eyes' and saying 'this isn't happening, I'm alright, I'm gonna be fine,' to actually say: 'OK, I feel shit.'"

Later – much later – as part of Jarvis's reappraisal of *This Is Hardcore* for the release of the Deluxe edition, Jarvis would reveal, 'I think the opening lines of "The Fear" best sum up *This Is Hardcore*. We've had our Pop Moment and this was our evocation of the aftermath. That we didn't flinch from doing that makes me proud'.

Recorded, like much of *This Is Hardcore*, between March '97 and January '98, at Townhouse and Olympic Studios, 'The Fear' is five and a half minutes of pain and beauty, and almost certainly the bravest and most honest song to kick off a record in the 1990s. And if you don't think Pulp knew exactly what they were doing when they recorded 'The Fear', consider this: on 7 September 1998, Pulp released 'Party Hard', the fourth single to be lifted from *This Is Hardcore*, and on its flip-side, you could find a seven minute mix of 'The Fear' called 'The Complete and Utter Breakdown Version'.

Oh, and one more thing: I'm sorry, Jarvis, but our time is up.

6
The Earth Is Where We Are

Except our time isn't really up, is it, since we have several more sessions scheduled.

So, let us continue.

Are small acts of heroism done in private more meaningful than visible achievements? On 'Dishes', Jarvis Cocker seems to think so.

> '"Dishes" came to me on the bike on the way to the rehearsal room', he told the April '98 edition of *Raygun* magazine. 'I often have ideas on the bike. It was about this conversation I'd had at about four o'clock in the morning once with this bloke who was saying that I was due for a mid-life crisis at 33, because that was the age that Jesus died. So, all men are supposed to get to 33, and then measure their achievements against Jesus's and obviously, you find yourself slightly second best. So, I was thinking about the way that when you're younger, you think the world revolves around you, and then thinking, "Well, maybe it doesn't."'[1]

So, there you have it. Except, I always thought Jesus was thirty-two when he died – as you can imagine, opinion is divided most vociferously on the subject – but I'll let that go for the moment.

'Dishes' is probably the most unambiguous song on *This Is Hardcore*, since it pretty much does what it says on the tin. By which I mean, it does exactly the opposite of what it says on the tin, since, presumably, you wouldn't find Jesus doing the dishes any time soon. 'I am not Jesus, though I have the same initials', croons Jarvis, and you can imagine his chuff-ness when he figured that out for the first time. Except, I've often wondered how much more chuffed he'd be if he'd commandeered the parable of Jesus and the loaves and fishes, just substituted 'dishes' for 'fishes', and then spent the rest of the song explaining how a little boy – young Jarvis perhaps? – had given five small loaves of bread and two small dishes to Jesus and watched him promptly feed over 5,000 people with leftovers to spare! Oh, how we would have all laughed. Or perhaps not, since Jarvis has bigger fish to fry.

'I am the man who stays home and does the dishes', continues Jarvis, barely acknowledging our attempt at humour. The phrase is spoken, rather than sung, over the top of some very simple, gentle piano chords, and you think, *Thank God! At least this sounds like Jarvis, 'cos apart from the Paul Daniels reference on the last one, I was beginning to have my doubts. Although, he's not really started singing yet, has he?* But this is almost certainly my point, since Jarvis's sing-speak has been well-known around these parts for many years, and one of the reasons why we think he might just be Britain's answer to Leonard Cohen. Or Sheffield's answer, at least. And, isn't that why he can shift from song to anecdote in the blink of an eye – both live and on record – with the ease of an acrobat?

And, of course, that last line from Jarvis makes you love him all the more. 'I was thinking', he explained at the time, 'that visible achievements like becoming famous… maybe in the public eye that's quite a big thing, but smaller kind of more mundane domestic things in a way are more heroic because there's no glory to be got from it – you don't get a round of applause for doing the dishes'. Jarvis would go on to expand further, suggesting that these 'heroic acts' were perhaps more meaningful than visible achievements done in public. 'You can get glory and applause and awards for things done in public', he told *Interview* magazine's Graham Fuller in July 1998, 'but you don't for just helping somebody out on a one-to-one level. You just do it for the sake of it, because you want to do it. That's what that song's trying to be about. I was really pleased with it.'[2]

'Dishes' is all chitter-chatter ladled over some sinister-but-gentle 1970's French elevator music, until the chorus arrives, when it becomes slightly more animated and we get some gently-ascending, distorted guitar framing more Jarvis pronouncements about dishes. 'I'd like to make this water wine but it's impossible', he intones, as some kind of apocalyptic mantra, before, 'I've got to get these dishes dry', reminding us once again that we are in his secular presence. "I'll read a story if it helps you sleep at night, I've got some matches if you ever need a light', he offers up in the next verse, a sentiment which Nick Hornby in his *Spin* magazine review of the album calls 'a reluctant redeemer's plea for recognition of his limitations'. 'The irony is', says Hornby, 'that any performer capable of providing such basic human services is always going to inspire more affection than anybody has a right to expect. If people love Jarvis, maybe it's because they feel the need for someone like him in their life: Who else is there who smiles back at you in quite the same way?'

If *This Is Hardcore*, as an album, offers a brutally honest look at humanity's dark side, then 'Dishes' surely stands alone as its only stab at redemption. It's another song about the fear of growing old, but it's straightforward, heart-breaking stuff at that, something that's borne out when the song has gone way past the limitations and inadequacies of its verse and chorus dateline, and is just cruising towards its conclusion. 'I'm not worried that I will never touch the stars', riffs Cocker, and never before have we heard someone so worried about never being able to touch the stars in our lives. The sentiment rivals Jon Waite's '(I Ain't) Missing You' for its *I'm not saying what I really mean* puff and bravado. 'Cos stars belong up in heaven, and the earth is where we are', continues Jarvis over the top of some gorgeous strings, and then a sparsely-plucked twelve-string guitar. But that 'Oh yeah' that Jarvis almost whispers at the end of this burst of inactivity is pure Pulp – pure Jarvis. It's just like the *oh yeahs* all over 'Babies' and 'F.E.E.L.I.N.G.C.A.L.L.E.D.L.OV.E'. Except it's nothing like them, really, is it? It's almost *resigned*, like a pale imitation of the *oh yeahs* we've come to love and respect, know and expect from Pulp. It says, *we've come a long way, baby, you and I, and anyway, 'aren't you happy just to be alive?'*

Jarvis once confessed that 'there might even have been a bit of the Michael Jackson thing' in "Dishes", cause he was setting himself up as that, and do you want to get crucified at the end of the day?'

To which, surely, there is only one response: *Old friend, we meet again.*

7
Nightclubbing

'Party Hard' has been accused of many things. The song 'explores the notion of your social life as a competitive sport, complete with injuries and of course, doping', said *Deluxe* magazine. It's just 'a cynical anthem' suggested *Access* magazine. *'It's about aging nightclubbers driving themselves to the brink of exhaustion to feel more "alive"'*, screamed *Rolling Stone*.[1] But the overriding accusation that haunts the song's very existence is that it's a Bowie-pastiche of some kind. Correspondingly – and in hindsight – the *Independent* would describe 'Party Hard' as both an 'homage to Bowie's *Station to Station* era, and a satire of the desperate compulsive hedonism that had devoured the Britpop scene'.[2] *Raygun* magazine called it ironic, which it is not – although presumably they meant the title, rather than the song itself – before going on to suggest it 'sees Jarvis at his most Bowie-esque, as the band boogie down at the *Scary Monsters* disco'. Similarly, the *NME's* Sylvia Patterson hailed it as 'the playboy's soundtrack, a bizarre, faintly idiotic *Scary Monsters* homage full of crisp observation'.[3] Subsequently, in the midst of a generally upbeat album review, *Select's* Roy Wilkinson went even further, maintaining that, '"Party Hard" sets Jarvis' meditation on joyless good times to a game but ersatz blast of stomping *Lodger*-period Bowie'.[4]

But is it? I mean, is it *Bowie-esque*, or even *Scary Monsters-esque*, for that matter? I suppose I get it, although since most critics can't work out what Bowie era Jarvis and Pulp are supposed to sound like here – *Scary Monsters, Lodger*, or in the case of the *Chicago Tribune*, 'a clever, catchy '90s take on the Bowie/Roxy/glam rock of the '70s' – I think we need to grant the band some leverage. Indeed, if anything, it's Iggy Pop's late '80s pop-edged output, rather than Bowie's work of the same era, that the song really reminds you of. And surely, Jarvis's voice is much closer to Iggy's loose baritone delivery than Bowie's gently-manicured rock vocals anyway?

No, it's Iggy's *Blah, Blah, Blah* that immediately springs to mind, as soon as 'Party Hard' kicks in. Released in 1986, and produced by Bowie – although unlike *The Idiot* and *Lust For Life*, which he also produced, Bowie didn't play any instruments on the record – *Blah, Blah, Blah* primarily features Bowie co-writes, as well as backing vocals by Bowie himself. There's been some debate about whether several tracks on *Blah, Blah, Blah* originated on Bowie's *Tonight* recordings two years earlier, as Bowie and Iggy collaborated on several songs on that record that didn't make the cut. **Ultimately**, Iggy would virtually disown *Blah, Blah, Blah*, calling it 'a Bowie album in all but name'. In any case, I think it's this Bowie-Iggy hybrid that permeates 'Party Hard' from the off. Well, that and the Steve Jones-infused guitar that Mark Webber employs to drive the song from start to finish.

Incidentally, ex-Sex Pistol Jones also co-wrote three songs and played guitar on *Blah, Blah, Blah*, but just to confuse the issue, I am equally prepared to admit that Jarvis could easily be doing a passable imitation of Edwyn Collins on 'Party Hard' instead – that is, if you consider that Edwyn Collins was doing a passable imitation of Iggy on his 1994 UK Top 50 chart-dodging track, 'A Girl Like You', in the first place. Or, perhaps he sounds exactly like Robert Palmer would sound – slightly bored, slightly amused – if he was singing about the vacuous nature of the parties that surrounded the music industry in the 1990s.

I'm glad you're still with me, since 'Party Hard' is that kind of song, dividing people to such an extent that some critics think it's the worst thing on *This Is Hardcore*. A darker 'Disco 2000', inspired by the band's dissatisfaction and exhaustion with clubbing, it may be, but does it – along with the rest of *Hardcore* – have 'none of rock's traditional dramatic glorification of mental and physical collapse'? *Select* magazine, huge supporters of Pulp and *This Is Hardcore* at the time, seemed to have an issue with 'Party Hard' in particular, suggesting 'the ennui, the meaninglessness, the endless melancholy is primped up with a dash of greasepaint, a swelling show-stopping chorus and the sense that, even now, the show must go on'.

"Jarvis leads us through a sombre tableau from the end of the party," said Roy Wilkinson. "The use of the utterly jaded, porn-fixated reveller as a metaphor for his own decline also works as a symbol of Britpop's drug-fuelled falling away. It's there in the way the title track details diminishing returns from ever more outré sex acts, but the epitome of this effect is 'Party Hard.'"

One of the oddest things about 'Party Hard' is that it's really just one long stream-of-consciousness verse all the way through, and any chorus you can detect is just the music for the verse broken up, with Jarvis chanting that 'Baby, you're driving me crazy' bit over the top. Of course, that's the bit that sounds like *Scary Monsters*, but it's important to understand why the song sounds like it does in the first place.

'It always had the title "Party Hard" after somebody once said it as a little phrase', Jarvis told *Deluxe* at the time. 'I found it hard to come up with something interesting to sing – Chris Thomas is quite a patient man, but he was kind of saying: "are you actually ever going to sing on this song or what?" So, under this pressure, I got this little Japanese guitar that's got batteries in it. I kind of got this tune that the melody goes against really – kind of flowed on top rather than part of the song. I got this idea of having two voices – two voices singing exactly the same words but there's this interval'.

In *Mother, Brother, Lover: Selected Lyrics* , published in 2011, Jarvis revealed that when Pulp had 'played a pretty horrendous corporate event in Barcelona in August 1996, in the run up to the concert one of the organisers informed us that he liked to party "pretty fucking hard"'. So that clarifies who the *somebody* is, but that *two voices* comment also explains the almost-undetectable delay/echo that accompanies Jarvis's vocals throughout the song.[5] It also goes some way towards explaining why Jarvis' perspective switches between first, second, and third person during different sections of the song, culminating in the use of that vocoder, just about the ideal robotic device to indicate multiple personalities – particularly, on those '*Baby*' refrains. And then, the song breaks down for a moment, before cantering towards its inevitable conclusion – 'When the party's over will you come home with me?' – an outro that's as close to 'Real Wild Child (Wild One)' and, yes, *Scary Monsters (and Super Creeps)* as it's allowed to be, without being pulled over by a policewoman for impersonating someone performing someone else's song.

Superficially, Jarvis Cocker is the star of 'Party Hard', but it's Steve Mackey's pulsating bassline and Mark Webber's brilliantly-monotone guitar parts that really steal the show. Indeed, despite its delusions of grandeur, and the fact that it's got its head in the clouds, 'Party Hard' is possibly Webber's finest hour on *Hardcore*, since, apart from the rather frightening, juddering keyboard and string interludes on the chorus, it's his rhythmic guitar – gloomy and desperate at times, all *Young Americans* funk at others – that drives the song. Not even Mackey and Webber's histrionics, however, can save 'Party Hard' from its *they-also-served* status amongst the echelons of polite *This Is Hardcore* society: cold and observational in tone, and regularly left out of any top twenty Pulp track lists, the years have not been kind to 'Party Hard'. Thankfully, the song neither knows nor cares what you think of it, and just stands there, looking blankly back at you, thinking about nothing and arranging its hair.

Released on 7 September 1998, 'Party Hard' became the fourth and final single to be lifted off *This Is Hardcore*, and spawned an excellent Mike Mills-directed video inspired by a tape of an old German variety show that the band had recently become enamoured with, featuring girls wearing tight Pulp T-shirts dancing around Cocker as the band mimed the song. B-sides of the single included 'We Are The Boyz' – the song Pulp had composed for Todd Haynes' film *Velvet Goldmine* – the Complete and Utter Breakdown Version of 'The Fear', Stretch 'n' Vern's 'Michel Lombert' remix, and a *Hardly Party Mix* of 'Party Hard' by All Seeing I, although several other mixes – including Chocolate Layers, Christopher Just, Tom Middleton Dub, and Tom Middleton Vocal – surfaced on various twelve-inch white label promos at the time.

'Party Hard' was Pulp's twenty-second single to date, and reached No. 29 in the UK charts – the band's lowest chart position since 'Do You Remember the First Time' back in March 1994. By this point in proceedings, *This Is Hardcore* had reached critical mass anyway, or as Island Records A&R executive Nigel Coxon suggested at the time: '"Party Hard" was as obvious a single on the record as anything, but it would have been hard whatever we put out after *Hardcore*. The album was … falling off and things had moved on, and I think whatever we'd have put out as a single would've struggled'.

8
Leave Your Wheelchair Outside

Rock stars have never dealt very well with the prospect of ageing. Indeed, most of the time, even the humdrum nature of survival gets short shrift. But nothing gets past Britain's unlikeliest popstar, Jarvis Cocker, who, emboldened by the inevitability of the ageing process, decided to write 'Help the Aged', a song that cocks its elderly leg at all that crap, and says, *We all get older, just get over it.*

Received wisdom suggests that 'Help the Aged' is a 'sarcastic' reflection on ageing – Jarvis was in his thirty-third year when he penned it – although, as he explained to *Hot Press* upon the album's release, it had quite specific origins.

> 'The song came from being on tour and having to sleep in these bunks on a coach', he revealed, 'which are kind of like the same dimensions as a coffin, so getting up in a coffin every night probably quite pissed makes you prone to maudlin thoughts. You can get slightly morbid. But the song is also a little bit cruel. It's just trying to get through that kind of sentimentality where you think of old people as people who are there to give you sweets on a Sunday. It's like they're a different species. One part of it came from

this Scottish bloke talking about living in some bad housing projects in Glasgow in the '30s, and he said that for kicks what they used to do, was get a hosepipe and run the gas through a pint of milk, and then drink the milk and it got you off your head. And that got me thinking. Everybody's kicking off about kids and their glue-sniffing, but people have always been doing it'.[1]

Despite Jarvis occasionally making light of such matters, 'Help the Aged' is anything but insubstantial, and quite definitely born out of a very real fear of dying. Speaking to Graham Fuller in July 1998, Jarvis would maintain that:

Everybody knows they're going to die eventually and nobody likes it – or the thought of getting older and not being able to do what you used to do. I think people are actually more scared of not being young anymore, than the thought of getting old. They don't perceive very much that's attractive about adulthood, so they extend their adolescence to ridiculous lengths, myself included. I guess when I first came up with the line, I found it a bit funny, but often my way of trying to deal with things I'm worried about is to turn them into a song, and instead of hide, confront them. Doing that hopefully helps me get through. I've always been aware of ageing, because success did come quite late to us, and it's difficult to hold onto your dignity in the pop-music business.

'Help The Aged' stands very much as an outlier as far as *This Is Hardcore* is concerned. It is, after all, the song that hastened Russell Senior's departure from the band, prompting the veteran guitarist to comment, '"Help the Aged", I didn't like and didn't feel involved with and tried to avoid being released. Jarvis was very keen on it and I guess we had musical differences'. Russell's comment, however, does force one to ask the question: *What kind of song would have made you stay in the band then? Another 'Common People'?*

The truth of the matter is that 'Help the Aged', whist hiding in plain sight as a blatant attempt at career sabotage, is easily the most heartfelt song on *This Is Hardcore*. 'I think the general feeling from the critics was kind of "It's good, but, ooh, it's not 'Disco 2000', is it?"' said drummer Nick Banks. 'They didn't quite understand it'. Scratch that; it's possibly the most heartfelt song on any rock album of the era. 'By the climax … the song is breaking your heart in ways you couldn't have anticipated', said Nick Hornby at the time. And so, the lyric, 'if you look very hard behind those lines upon their face, you may see where you are headed, and it's such a lonely place', becomes one of the loneliest lines you could ever listen to without crying.

Except, you *are* crying, aren't you? And when Cocker sings about *existential loneliness*, he is really doing something that very few popstars have done before or since: singing about the elderly with compassion and sincerity. Perhaps Elvis Costello came close with 'Veronica', a song co-written with Paul McCartney about Costello's grandmother who experienced severe memory loss, or Tori Amos with '16 Shades of Blue', or even Grateful Dead with 'Touch of Grey', but even these attempts to transmogrify the listener into a state of empathy fall short when put up against 'Help the Aged'. Indeed, whist Cocker may have idly dismissed 'Help the Aged' to the *NME* as 'just me whining on about getting old' – well, they started it! – he's not getting away with it that easily, since we all know what he's up to. Or as *The Los Angeles Times* put it, 'In "Help the Aged", sentiments that might sound cynical from someone else are full of compassion, and the simple knowledge that we all get older'.[2]

Musically, 'Help the Aged' is like Radiohead's 'Creep', or at least it starts quietly with some gentle piano-tinkling from Candida, and some even gentler musings on mortality and the inevitability of growing older from Jarvis – 'don't just put them in a home, can't have much fun in there all on their own' – before clanging guitars, layered harmonies, and pounding beats herald the arrival of the most unlikely chorus – 'In the meantime we try, try to forget that nothing lasts forever' – where Jarvis has become as vocally ravaged as the best of them. 'No big deal', yelps Cocker, except it is. 'Pulp reach out to the inevitable with a mixture of resignation, compassion and humour', said *Rolling Stone* at the time, 'and package it all in a mirror ball of florid strings, helium-enriched vocal harmonies and shimmering guitars'.

'Help the Aged' spawned a cute-as-heck video featuring Pulp performing in an old folks' home whilst young men dressed up to look like elderly men flirt with much younger women. 'We decided it'd be better to use young people made up to look old than to use actual old people', Jarvis explained, 'as if, for some reason, looking old had become trendy'. The video was inspired by Powell and Pressburger's 1946 classic movie, *A Matter of Life and Death,* and features Jarvis singing the first few verses – the quiet bits – whilst riding a Stannah stairlift up to the first floor of the old folks' home where the band performs, before they all continue their journey skywards to the after-life, where they perform once again. Interestingly, Stannah rejected the initial plan of riding the stairlift to heaven on the grounds that they did not want to be associated with death, which begs the question: *Had they actually listened to the words of the song?*

'Help the Aged' was released on 11 November 1997, and came backed with 'Tomorrow Never Lies' and 'Laughing Boy' – inspired by 'a houseguest from Iceland who overstayed his welcome', Jarvis wrote in *Mother, Brother, Lover* – a rather maudlin affair featuring some delightful, what-sounds-like lap-steel guitar. Both of these songs were included on the eighty-six minute long double-vinyl release in March 1998. The single reached No. 8, thus making it Pulp's fifth Top Ten hit in a row. 'I was really pleased when it got to number eight', insisted Jarvis. 'Maybe we overestimated people's willingness to confront their own mortality in a pop record, but I'm proud that we got a record about getting old and dying into the Top Ten'. Yet the band's entire world had been turned upside down since the release of their previous Top Ten hit: Russell Senior had left the building, Steve and Nick had both fathered sons, Mark had endured a traumatic split from his girlfriend, and Candida had lost her brother to an Indian religious sect. And Jarvis? Well, he was half-way up his ladder to the unknown.

'Pop music traditionally deals with young flash things', Jarvis told Radio 1, 'but pop music itself is middle-aged. I just want to find a way of being an adult without it being boring. I don't wanna continue acting like a teenager for the rest of my life because I can't hack it'. And then much later, to the *NME*'s Roger Morton, he continues:

People are desperately gripping on to their youth into their thirties, which 20 years ago would have been quite unheard of. And because of the so-called youth revolution in the Sixties, still all the images of what's to be desired in life are based around young, fit-looking people. So, it's going to end up causing lots of problems because the brutal fact of it is that the ageing process is something that no one is immune to. Everybody gets old and everybody dies.

'Help the Aged' was the oldest song on *This Is Hardcore* – 'I was beginning to feel like if we didn't get it out soon, it'd be past its sell-by date', said Jarvis at the time – but on Halloween night in 1997, eleven days before its release, Jarvis dedicated the song to his father when introducing it to the audience at the La Monte Young benefit. Three months later, with the release date of *This Is Hardcore* little more than a month away, he would travel to Australia to meet his father, for the first time in more than twenty-five years.

9
This Is Barry

This Is Hardcore's title track is vulgar and shockingly explicit. It's also a sublime masterpiece. Kicking off like a funereal update of Ravel's *Bolero*, Jarvis doesn't actually start singing until a minute and thirty in, and then, once he's bothered to turn up, he doesn't actually sound like Jarvis at all. It is Pulp's answer to 'Paranoid Android' and The Verve's 'Bitter Sweet Symphony'. Only better. The *New Musical Express* called it 'possibly the creepiest single released by a commercial artist in recorded history', before concluding, 'it's awful. And brilliant'.[1] *The Guardian* suggested, 'it's as grim as they come', before putting it at No. 6 on their 'Pulp All Time Top Ten Songs' list.[2] Upon release, *AllMusic* hailed it as 'a frightening monument to weary decadence', whilst in 2013 *Stereogum* suggested 'the song's parts are alternatively some of the dirtiest and saddest sounds to ever make it into a Pulp song'.[3] Twenty-five years later, the *Independent* would compare it to 'James Bond playing strip poker in a sex dungeon'.

I must admit that when I heard the song for the first time – I was sitting in the offices of Rough Trade whilst Pulp managers Geoff Travis and Jeanette Lee played it to me and John Best – I sat there open-mouthed, thinking, *So, this is the single then?*

There were finer divisions, of course. '"This Is Hardcore" is the song I'm most proud of on the album', said Steve Mackey, explaining:

> I think it's the best song we've ever written. If only in that song alone, we've achieved enough that makes this album important to me. That song has made it all worthwhile because we've stretched ourselves, and done something that – to me – still sounds exciting one year later.

Meanwhile, Mark Webber said,

> I was never a very big fan of the song. I can appreciate that it's good work, but I never really liked it from the outset. Jarvis didn't want people to expect an album of 'Common People' and 'Disco 2000'. He wanted to redraw the boundaries, and recently it's been a case of Jarvis' will overriding everyone else's common sense.

And Jarvis?

> "It started off as an experiment," he said. "I was really pleased with it because I'd been thinking vaguely before doing this record to get away from the verse-chorus-verse-middle-bit-double-chorus-end kind of structure but still have a melody . . . we kind of achieved it on that song."

So what's all the fuss about?

'This Is Hardcore' centres around a sample of 'Bolero on the Moon Rocks' by the Peter Thomas Sound Orchestra – in the same way that The Verve's 'Bitter Sweet Symphony' centres around a sample from a 1965 orchestral version of the Rolling Stones song 'The Last Time' – which German composer Thomas composed for the 1966 television science fiction series, *Raumpatrouille – Die phantastischen Abenteuer des Raumschiffes Orion*, or *Space Patrol – The Fantastic Adventures of the Spaceship Orion*. It's remarkable, therefore, that the original 'Bolero on the Moon Rocks' clip from the soundtrack manages to sound both sinister and porn-laden at the same time, perhaps a result of Cocker *jigsawing* the sample through the pornographic themes and the creepy, profoundly uneasy-listening landscape of the song.

The song kicks off with some super-simple drums – like on an instruction tape – before *that* sample kicks in, and we get some deceptively simple yet ominous piano doodles – again, like on an instruction tape – from Candida Doyle, and some even more ominous-sounding horns. We're in a late-night jazz club, or worse, a seedy strip den. It's like Portishead, actually, magnificent and *stirring*. Then the song seems to stop, except it doesn't stop at all; it's just idling along waiting for something to happen. And then it does.

'You are hardcore, you make me hard', sings Cocker, and you suddenly think, *Oh my god, he's gone and done it now. He said it, he actually said it.* 'It seems I saw you in some teenage wet dream, I like your get up if you know what I mean', he continues, and now you're thinking, *if we make a run for it whilst he's distracted, he may not notice we were here at all. But if he does, the consequences could be catastrophic.* And whilst all this is going on, those ominous-sounding horns come back in again, and Jarvis sounds quite excited – so excited, in fact, that when he says, 'I wanna make a movie, so let's star in it together', you can't help noticing that the song has just exploded like a machine gun.

RAT-A-TAT-TAT.
Action.

Ostensibly, 'This Is Hardcore' is about a man realising his sexual fantasy for a woman by making a pornographic movie with her, and it's interesting to note how Jarvis has finally stepped out from behind the curtains to be both director and star, a player in an industry you wouldn't normally expect to find him in. Hey, it's called *disengaged cynicism*, doncha know? Although Jarvis was keen to explain to *Raygun's* Michael Krugman in April 1988:

> It's like when I first started going out with girls and stuff, and finding it very hard to express myself, because anything you said sounded like a line from a film. Films and TV give you an impression of knowing something about the world or knowing something about situations. But they only show them, they don't communicate what they're actually like. They're no substitute for actually doing it. That leaves you feeling kind of prematurely jaded and a bit jaundiced about things. So when it came to making this record, suddenly it was a bit like *The Purple Rose of Cairo*, where the audience becomes part of the film. All my life I've been an observer, not only of films and TV, but of life, and then as soon as you get that germ of public acceptance, then you are somebody else's show. You're actually part of the action on the screen. That's why there's a bit of an obsession with it on the record. It's comparing what it was like as a spectator and what it's like being part of the action, and that's always going to be a bit of a disappointment.

He's not kidding, right? As 'This Is Hardcore' progresses relentlessly towards its despairing conclusion, via several John Barry-tinged episodes and skirmishes – much of the melodrama is provided by Nicolas Dodd's orchestrations and Anne Dudley's shimmering strings – we catch Jarvis yelping, 'You can't be a spectator, oh no, you got to take these dreams & make them whole', before finally getting to hear the most dramatic and frightening guitar solo this side of a Spiritualized convention, like *The Twilight Zone* through a Fuzz Box, or the Bernard Butler guitar solo on Suede's 'The Asphalt World'. And then, we're suddenly through to the other side, and it's beautiful, except Jarvis is saying, 'It's what men in stained raincoats pay for, but in here it is pure', and finally, 'Oh, that goes in there', and you're not quite sure if you heard that correctly, but there it is again several times.

And then it's over.

'Hardcore pornography is the brick wall at the end of this kind of tunnel', Jarvis told *Hot Press* in July 1998, elaborating:

> If all the romance is stripped away, it becomes just a physical process, and you realise that. . . in some ways, you're constantly trying to strip this stuff away, all the artifice and the veils, and when you get to the end of it, to the actual thing, you want to put all the clothes back on it, because it's all a bit repulsive in a way. That's really what that song, and the record as a whole is trying to get at, that maybe you do have to keep a bit of distance from things. Hardcore porn has a brutalising effect.

The killer message in 'This Is Hardcore' is in its penultimate line, 'What exactly do you do for an encore?' It's a rhetorical question, of course, about the aftermath – the debris, if you will – of the sexual act, primarily for a man. The *NME*, in a cover story trailed 'Inside the Filthy Mind of Jarvis Cocker', called the song a 'brooding seven-minute epic about sexual psychosis and the sour aftertaste which fame leaves at the back of your throat, a sombre bloated behemoth which doesn't so much sing along with the Common People as shaft them violently up the arse', and whilst that's a charming observation, there's more to this than meets the eye. *That* line is surely Jarvis's attempt at redemption, in all sorts of ways.

> 'It's the feeling that you've done it all, or exhausted every variation', Jarvis suggested at the time. 'And I'm not just talking about a sexual thing here. Then you say, "Well, what do you do for an encore?" Maybe that was a question that I was asking meself a lot whilst we were actually making the record. But it answered itself really because we made another album.'

It's also about what one is supposed to do after something called the *Michael Jackson Incident* has thrown you to the wolves.

'This Is Hardcore' is about revulsion and attraction at the same time, or 'doing something that you know is wrong', as Jarvis told Sean Plummer in May 1998, 'but kind of getting a kick out of it', although the *NME*'s Sylvia Patterson suggested the song was 'an operatic opus of staggeringly bleak refrain; a paean to a pornographic fantasy as a metaphor for fatal fame'. It wasn't until much later, however, that Jarvis would count the song as one of the best things Pulp had ever done.

'Whether it was worth the grief it took to get there', he told *Mojo* five years after its release, 'and the psychological landscape I had to inhabit to write it, I dunno. I was losing it. It wasn't a good commercial move, and there was the terrible realisation that at this point of psychic and spiritual disintegration, the spectre of Paul Daniels appears to haunt you. I got drunk and wrote the words, then looked at them the next day but couldn't remember having written them. It was the same in the recording studio. I got really hammered and sung it, and can't really remember singing it either. It was obviously in me but it took a lot to get it out. That's what gives it something slightly unearthly; it's unhealthy, sort of glossy and shiny but in a kind of queasy way. Island must have been horrified. To their credit they did get behind it – the video must have cost a quarter of a million pounds.'[4]

Ah, *that* video, undoubtedly – along with the Beastie Boys' 'Sabotage' – the best video for a pop or rock song ever made. And, as Jarvis points out, not cheap. Filmed at Pinewood Studios and based around the premise of an unfinished Hollywood B-movie, the six-and-a-half-minute film is directed by Doug Nichol and produced by John Moule, and features the band amongst several other actors recreating vintage Hollywood scenes, including a sprawling dance sequence where Jarvis shuffles through a collection of gold-lamé swim-suited dancers and turquoise-plumed feathers. It's a feathery nod to Busby Berkeley, whose 1943 film musical, *The Gang's All Here,* was charged with sexual innuendo and erotica after depicting dozens of scantily clad women handling very large bananas, as well as some opening and closing waterlily vaginas. Nichol's homage to Berkeley is just about the perfect fit.

'I really love those things because they're so artificial and they could only exist for the camera', Jarvis told *Hot Press* when discussing the 'Hardcore' video. 'And yet there's something very moving about those Busby Berkeley films'. Later, in the same article, whilst talking about the sequence where Jarvis and a leading lady are seen 'driving' in their red car, he'd say:

> Technicolour was like the apex of that thing in those big Hollywood films of the late '50s where everything was artificial. You would never get colours like that in nature and, every time somebody got in a car it was done with rear projection. It's all completely stylised and I suppose a lot of the time our songs are about trying to get underneath that surface of what the things really are, but at the same time really liking that stuff.

And then, when discussing Busby Berkeley again, he'd muse:

> What I've kind of worked out is that he does these things where real people are making these fantastic kinds of kaleidoscopic patterns in real time, all working together making this beautiful shape, so it seems very harmonious. Then he always gets a kind of close shot, where he goes along the chorus line and you see the individual girls' faces, and they're not like fantastic beauties or anything, but they create this beautiful thing that can only ever exist for the camera. If you were there watching it happen, it

wouldn't be the same thing. So that's why I was really glad that we managed to get that routine in at the end of the video.

Interestingly, although the Berkeley themes are writ large in the 'Hardcore' video, the actual inspiration for the film was a book called *Still-Life*, edited by Diane Keaton and Marvin Heiferman. The book contains photographs of stills and publicity shots of films produced in Hollywood between 1940 and 1969. Many of the scenes in the video reproduce specific stills from the book, substituting members of Pulp for actors.

'This Is Hardcore' became the second single to be lifted off the album, although as the album had yet to be released, I think 'lifted' is stretching it a bit. Backed with 'Ladies Man' and the sleaze-ladled 'The Professional', and armed with several alternative remixes of the title track across the formatting spectrum, 'This Is Hardcore' was released on 16 March 1998, and reached No. 12 in the UK singles chart. 'I think it's got a place', said bassist Steve Mackey upon release. 'To me "This Is Hardcore" is like a challenge in a song, it's a gauntlet for the rest of the year. It's like when Radiohead put out "Paranoid Android" in 1997: here you are, deal with this'. And that's with the proviso that 'This Is Hardcore' was very nearly not called 'This Is Hardcore' at all.

'When we write a song, we always give them titles because the lyrics are always the last thing to happen', Jarvis told *Raygun* in 1998. 'Some we have working titles to refer to things and they're usually stupid. "Love Scenes" became "Seductive Barry", "Hardcore" was called "Barry", Barry

was a big character on this record. One song was called
"Barry Swings". And then we had "Seductive Barry". We
could have called the record *This Is Barry*.'

'I can't believe it took me this long', howls Jarvis towards
the end of the song. It had only been twenty years, but I think
we know what he means.

10
A Hangover without End

I can't pretend that 'TV Movie' is my favourite song on *This Is Hardcore*. In fact, it's not even my favourite song called 'TV Movie'. And to make matters worse, it's not even my favourite song called 'TV Movie' that was made publicly and legally available that year, since that particular honour has to go to Bruce Springsteen, who included his song 'TV Movie' – a song that had only existed as a bootleg for several years after he wrote and recorded it back in 1982 – on his *Tracks* box set in 1998. In contrast, Jarvis Cocker, maintains that Pulp's song of the same name, 'is like a TV movie with just some kind of plot for the sake of it, and cardboard characters and nothing connecting. Just the kind of thing that fills in time on a TV station'. He went on to suggest:

> You can always spot a TV movie when it's coming on the telly just by the titles. I don't know how they do it. It must be some process. When I was an adolescent growing up, my main introduction to seeing naked women and stuff was on the TV. If you got a foreign art film on BBC2, after 11 o'clock, you could be probably guaranteed of seeing something.

All of which persuades me to wonder what point I was trying to make in the first place. So, no change there then.

The bleakest song amongst *A Catalogue of Bleak Songs*, Pulp's 'TV Movie' is a lament to the end of a relationship. 'Without you my life has become a hangover without end, a movie made for TV: bad dialogue, bad acting, no interest', moans Jarvis, and musically, it feels like we are in 'Something Changed' territory – except this is 'Something Changed' gone wrong. Correspondingly, if 'Something Changed' – the fourth and final single to be released from *Different Class* in March 1996 – was about the random nature of how important events happen in life, then 'TV Movie' is about how those random events might not always conjure up the sort of delightful eventualities you would want to write home about. And whilst 'Something Changed' elicited praise from the likes of *Rolling Stone* – 'delightfully cheesy loser's-lounge blend of strings and low, throaty guitar twang' – and retrospectively *Pitchfork* – 'a straightforwardly romantic and gorgeously touching song about the unknown and unknowable turning points in anyone's life' – you can't quite imagine 'TV Movie' eliciting such charmingly-reflective ruminations. Cocker maintains of 'Something Changed' that he's 'been stopped by a lot of people who tell me that song was played at their wedding. They walked down the aisle to it'. But 'TV Movie' at a wedding? I don't think so.

And yet, they're both swooning, lumbering, cumbersome, masochistic, needy and largely acoustic numbers that are just begging to be loved. *Melody Maker* was forced to hail 'TV Movie' as 'a softly beautiful torch song', but you can't help but notice that the song is really just a love-gone-wrong song about not being able to write a song about love-going-wrong. Billy Joel's 'Famous Last Words' treads similar ground – '*These are the last words I have to say, that's why it took so long to write*' – and in the end, it's the extraordinarily beautiful set of lyrics accompanying 'TV Movie' that warrants the song's inclusion on the album in the first place. Indeed, when Nick Hornby, whilst writing about *This Is Hardcore* in *Spin*, suggested that 'England's unofficial poet laureate Jarvis Cocker perfects his poetry of the prosaic', he could easily be writing *only* about 'TV Movie', rather than the album as a whole.

On 23 May 2008, at the Brighton Dome, as part of the Brighton Festival, and more than ten years after the release of *This Is Hardcore*, Jarvis Cocker delivered a specially commissioned lecture to 1,800 people on the role of lyrics in popular music.[1] The 135-minute lecture was particularly noteworthy for the way in which Jarvis illustrated the differences between lyrics and poetry. As part of the lecture, he made the, admittedly-obvious, point, that 'lyrics are different to poetry because poetry is standalone whereas lyrics are part of something else: the song'. What was most intriguing, however, was Jarvis's insistence that whatever lyrics are – and it is his contention that just because lyrics and poetry are different, doesn't mean to say that songs can't have a poetic quality – he prefers to see them presented as prose – as a single block of text – rather than as poetry. Notwithstanding the fact that I wanted this book to be a single block of text until my publishers intervened, Jarvis further contends that 'when lyrics are presented like this, they're far more neutral and unimposing', hence the message on Pulp's record sleeves that says, 'N.B. Please do not read the lyrics whilst listening to the recordings'. Jarvis continues:

> If you read them whilst listening to the recordings, you're extracting the lyrics from their natural habitat – when you read words from a page, it's different to them as part of a song. When you're listening to a song, the lyrics are subservient to the rhyme. Whereas if you read them off a page, they have a natural rhythm.

To be honest for a moment – it's a glimpse of the real me – I can't think of a better song than 'TV Movie' to actually dispute Jarvis's point about lyrics not being able to stand alone. Not that I have any issues with his contention as a whole – and notice I say *dispute* not *disprove* – it's just that 'TV Movie' is the kind of song whose lyrics absolutely stand up as poetry – whatever that is – and make me love the song, in spite of the fact that I am not particularly smitten by its musical charms. But then again, when Jarvis suggests elsewhere, that 'lyrics don't really matter – they're an optional extra, much like a sunroof or a patio. But when music and lyrics work together, they're better than the sum of parts', he could easily be talking about 'TV Movie'.

There's a weird kind of radio interference that pervades 'TV Movie'. It starts and ends the song, and it's deliberately haunting. Perhaps we're listening into 'TV Movie' on another line? When Jarvis sings, 'Is it a kind of weakness to miss someone so much, to wish the day would go away, like you did yesterday?' he's never sounded more like Leonard Cohen. And then, just when the song really gets interesting, he starts whistling. People whistle for all sorts of reasons – to help calm themselves when in danger or distress, or to distract attention away from something that they are doing – but there's only one reason why Jarvis decides to whistle halfway through 'TV Movie': he wants to communicate feelings which cannot be expressed in words.

Just like he'd been trying to tell us all along.

11
Letters Home

Utterly heart-breaking, 'A Little Soul' is a letter of ill-disguised remorse, addressed from Cocker's father to his estranged son. Written in the latter part of 1997, the song actually prompted Cocker Jr. to visit his father in Australia the following year, for the first time in twenty-eight years. 'It was weird', he told *Hot Press* in July 1998, 'as soon as I'd written the song, I knew that I'd have to go and see him. Did it help me understand him a bit more? I don't think I'll ever understand meself'.

Later, in *Mother, Brother, Lover: Selected Lyrics*, Jarvis revealed:

'My housemate's father died suddenly and it made me think about my own father, who had left home when I was seven years old and who I had not seen since apart from a brief visit when I was twelve.'

George Malcolm 'Mac' Cocker was born in Sheffield in 1941. Variously, a local jazz musician, an occasional actor, and an Australian radio announcer who worked for the Australian Broadcasting Corporation radio network for thirty-three years between 1974 and 2007, Mac had married Jarvis's mother Christine in the early 1960s, before Christine gave birth to Jarvis in 1963, and then his sister Saskia some three years later. Then, one morning in 1970, the family found a note letting them all know Mac had walked out on them. He subsequently moved to Sydney, Australia, where, for several years thereafter, he claimed to be the brother of Sheffield-born singer and musician Joe Cocker.

In November 1998, eight months on from the release of *This Is Hardcore*, Christine Connolly gave an interview to the *Daily Mirror* revealing that when she 'woke up to find that Mac had deserted us, I was totally devastated'.[1] She continued, 'Being left with two young children to bring up, well, it put me off men for a while, but I never tried to turn my kids against their father.' Much later, in December 2006, Jarvis would tell the *Independent*'s Hermione Eyre that he had forgiven his father.[2] 'I don't feel any bitterness towards him at all', he said, 'I feel sorry for him'. Eighteen months before that, in June 2007, upon his retirement from the airwaves, Mac Cocker perhaps gave a flavour of his life in Australia when he told *ABC Local*:

'Since I started here in 1990, I have done every shift on 105.7 ABC Darwin' – he'd left Australia in 1985, to travel the world for five years – 'but one of my favourite memories of these times was broadcasting the Globetrotter from the Mindil Beach Markets on Sunday afternoons. I remember sitting there one afternoon and this couple from Haiti came over. I was playing Bookman Experience at that moment and they asked me in a kind of baffled voice if that was Kompass music (which is traditional Haitian music). Bookman Experience was banned in Haiti and they were amazed.'[3]

In 1996, at the height of Cocker Jr's fame, an Australian newspaper tracked down Cocker Sr. to Darwin, Australia, before *The Sun* picked up on the story and offered to fly Jarvis to Australia to effect a reunion. 'I can't imagine anything worse', he said at the time, but in February 1998, once 'A Little Soul' and *This Is Hardcore* were done and dusted, Jarvis and Saskia did indeed travel over to the Northern Territory to meet their father, an encounter Jarvis was persuaded to discuss with *Arena's* Paul Morley, less than six weeks later:

> This is a theory that I've come up with over the past few weeks . . . maybe because of my father leaving when I was young, and all the fathers round my way did a similar thing, it was as if they were all sat in the pub one night and they all decided to fuck off at once. With my father leaving, maybe that made me think that I didn't want to travel in a straight line or anything. I decided to act in a more exaggerated kind of way because I didn't want to take life seriously. It seemed to me that if you took your life too seriously, like me father, then you ended up in the kind of mess that I wasn't prepared to be involved in. The rigmarole of day-to-day life seemed to go nowhere. Which is kind of a contradiction in terms considering as I've ended up writing about that kind of everyday life. Maybe I'm fascinated with the everyday because I've never been able to do it.

And then, when *Melody Maker's* Robin Bresnark quizzed him further about the reunion in a piece to coincide with the single release of 'A Little Soul', Jarvis went on:

It's just difficult. You don't know what to feel. You think it should be a big deal, 'cos obviously he's somebody that a lot of your personality comes from, but you don't know him at all. So, at once there's a real closeness, but also a real awkwardness 'cos you're not sure how to behave. They are a stranger to you, really. But I don't like to talk about it, ' cos it is something very personal. I would hate it if, by talking about it, I kind of spoilt it.

Three months later, in a September 1998 piece timed to coincide with the start of Pulp's Australian tour, Mac Cocker revealed to Paul Ham of *The Sunday Times*:

They stayed with me for six days, and we thrashed out a few things. Both my children are now adults and they asked a lot of questions. I was at pains to give them the correct answers. The encouraging thing is that the meeting did not close the doors.[4]

'A Little Soul' was described by *Select* magazine as one of the less distressed songs on *This Is Hardcore* – 'a gorgeous, mid-paced, Memphis-tinged imagined appeal to Jarv from his errant daddy' – but the first thing you notice about this disconsolately beautiful ode to bad parenting is how much it reminds you of Smokey Robinson and the Miracles' 'Tracks of My Tears'. Of course, subject-wise, the two songs could hardly be more different – one is telling a story about a man who is trying to hide his pain, but cannot conceal the tracks made by his tears, whilst the other tells a story from the point of view of the singer's father who is trying to hide the pain he has inflicted upon his children after one day walking out on them. Hang on a second, you can't fool me! Aren't they both just trying to say the same thing by not saying anything at all really? The words 10cc and 'I'm Not in Love' immediately spring to mind, but when Smokey Robinson first looked in the mirror and conjured up 'Tracks of My Tears', wasn't he just doing exactly what Cocker Jr. was doing many years later, when he wrote 'A Little Soul' and saw the face of his father staring back at him?

In April 1998, Jarvis Cocker told the *Observer*'s Lynn Barber, that his mother was 'as close to a Bohemian as it's possible to get in Sheffield'. Later, as part of the same piece, Barber pointed out that his father's premature departure from the family home meant that Jarvis became 'entirely surrounded by women – his mother, his sister, his grandmother, his aunt, his great aunt', and perhaps, it's this observation that gets to the heart of the matter: 'How come you treat your woman so bad?' begins 'A Little Soul', and then, a little later, 'You see your mother and me, we never got along that well you see'. It's heart-rending stuff, and when Jarvis sings, 'You look like me but please don't turn out like me', there's not a dry eye in the house.

There's some terrific guitar skulduggery on 'A Little Soul' – particularly the solo at 2:22 minutes in. Anne Dudley's string arrangements are also worth the entry price alone, but it's the song's conflicting sentimentality that overrides proceedings at every turn. At one point, as the set-up to the kiss-off line at the end of the first chorus – 'I've only got a little soul' – Jarvis sings, 'I had one, two, three, four shots of happiness', and then, as the set-up to the song's denouement, he sings 'I have run away from the one thing that I ever made', and it's this ongoing redemption plotline that carries the song along. 'No, I don't feel bitter at all', Jarvis confessed when Barber pressed him further on the subject of his father:

> I understand it totally. If you think about that time, the 1960s, and I know that I wasn't a planned pregnancy so, for a start, he probably didn't want to get married. Then, I know he had aspirations to be a musician and to be an actor, which probably had to be put on hold. And also, he ended up living next door to my mother's parents – and they're nice people but, you know, it probably made him feel just a bit under pressure.

Talk about forgiveness.

In the video for 'A Little Soul' – directed by Hammer and Tongs at Olympic Studios – much younger 'double' versions of Pulp are dismissed by their real-life counterparts, as there's always something more interesting or less-taxing for the band members to be doing instead: Steve is too busy playing video-games to notice mini-Steve; Nick is reading a magazine as his drums are pushed in front of him, his foot placed on a bass pedal, by his younger counterpart; Candida, asleep on an armchair, is pushed into the middle of the room, down a corridor and onto a stage, where her 'daughter' actually plays the piano for her; and Mark's guitar is carried upstairs and plugged into his amp for him by his 'son'. Whilst all this is going on, Jarvis's mini-me is busy making him cups of tea and being ignored whilst miming the words to the song. Considering Jarvis's 'son' is singing back the lyrics to him, which Jarvis had written for his dad to sing back to him, the whole thing is either the most ridiculously meta thing imaginable, or completely nonsensical. Of course, either way, it's quite brilliant.

Released on 8 June 1998, 'A Little Soul' was Pulp's twenty-first single, debuting at No. 22 in the UK charts. B-sides included, 'Like a Friend', the collaboration they'd written with Patrick Doyle for director Alfonso Cuaron's remake of *Great Expectations* – the song was also used in the Season 4 finale of *The Venture Bros*, and the *Daria* episode, 'Depth Takes A Holiday', but didn't make its live debut until Glastonbury in 2011, and since become a live stalwart – and the instrumental 'That Boy's Evil', originally released as a white label vinyl by Cocker and Mackey's side project The Chocolate Layers. Another B-side, 'Cocaine Socialism', was already living a life elsewhere as the album cut 'Glory Days', but with different lyrics.

12
Cartoons From Other People's Lives

Jarvis Cocker has been writing about what it feels like to be a man for as long as I can remember. Or rather, he's been trying to avoid writing about it, since, presumably, it's one of the most difficult things to write about if you're a man. More often than not, it'll be part of some oddly-envisaged sexual encounter – '*I don't care if you screw him, oh, just as long as you save a piece for me*' ('Do You Remember The First Time?') or 'The night was ending, he needed her undressed, he said he loved her, she tried to look impressed' ('O.U.') – but, over the years, Cocker has embedded himself so deeply into the characters that inhabit his songs, that it's sometimes difficult to know where Jarvis Cocker begins and where Jarvis Cocker ends. For instance, I'm pretty sure the protagonist in 'I Spy' who says 'Grass is something you smoke, birds are something you shag' is not Jarvis, but earlier on in the song, when he says, 'the crowd gasp at Cocker's masterful control of the bicycle', we may as well be all back to square one. Oh, he's the Scarlet Pimpernel, alright, rock music's most elusive superhero.

'I write a lot of songs from a woman's perspective', Jarvis told *Attitude* magazine's Martin Aston in November 1995, 'and a lot of songs are addressed to women as well. I think it's something to do with me being brought up by women, as there were no blokes around at all, except me grandad who was 60-odd and didn't really count. What I learnt about sex was from eavesdropping on my mother's friends having conversations in the kitchen, in the afternoon after I'd come home from school. So all snippets of information were of the female view. My mother had to teach me how to shave, which was funny because she'd never done it before.'[1]

So, what are we to make of 'I'm a Man'? Or rather, when it comes to being a man, what was Jarvis Cocker's frame of mind – and reference – in 1997, when he wrote it?

A year later, in July 1998, he told Graham Fuller, that just after the band finished recording 'Dishes', he:

'went to see that film *Nil by Mouth*, which is very harrowing, and it made me really glad I'd written that song because they seemed to key in with each other. The man in the film is so brutal and so unwilling to connect with his wife in any way. It's not really Oasis's fault but there's been this whole new lads' thing in the UK that has endorsed treating women like shit again. At first it was a kind of semi-ironic thing that followed political correctness, but in the end, it got taken on board and then turned into thuggery. *Nil by Mouth* showed where all that leads.'

Ah, yes, Oasis. Indeed, it's difficult to underestimate the influence of Noel, Liam and co. upon British lad culture in the 1990s. By April 1994, Suede may have (unknowingly) already played their last ever gig with Bernard Butler on guitar – at the Queens Hall, Edinburgh in February that year – as Blur were just about to release *Parklife*, while Pulp was celebrating the release of their fourth album, *His 'n' Hers* with nothing more than tea and cakes. By which I mean to say, that whilst *His 'n' Hers* included songs with titles like 'Lipgloss', 'Have You Seen Her Lately', and 'She's a Lady', Oasis had just released their debut single, 'Supersonic'. And can you imagine Oasis ever releasing a song called 'Acrylic Afternoons'?

One month later, in May 1994, *Loaded* magazine launched, alongside the strapline, 'for men who should know better', and rapidly – 'Acrylic Afternoons' aside – the 1990s started to become a toxic environment for women. A year later, Elastica would release their self-titled debut album, enabling Liam Gallagher to suggest, 'he wouldn't kick' singer Justine Frischmann out of bed, and by the end of the '90s, two British films, *Snatch* and *Lock, Stock and Two Smoking Barrels* – movies you could perhaps accuse of embracing lad culture – ruled the multiplexes.

Many years later, the National Union of Students, in conjunction with the University of Sussex, would put together a report entitled, 'That's what she said: Women's experiences of "lad culture" in higher education', and reference academic John Benyon's analysis, which highlights how the magazine *Loaded* 'consciously reduced working class masculinities to jokes, interest in cars and the objectification of women, and dismissed criticisms as humourless attacks on free speech which failed to see the ironic nature of the representations'.[2]

By 1995, *Melody Maker*'s Paul Lester was asking, 'Are we finally allowed to admit, post-*Loaded*, to admiring the female form?'[3] To which Jarvis replied, 'Well, it's a lot nicer to look at than the male form, isn't it?' But as far back as 1991, *GQ* had issued a press-release stating, 'GQ is proud to announce that the New Man has officially been laid to rest (if indeed he ever drew breath). The Nineties man knows who he is, what he wants and where he's going and he's not afraid to say so. And yes, he still wants to get laid', and by August 1996 – a month before Pulp landed the Mercury Music Prize for *Different Class* – Michael Bracewell perfectly summarised proceedings in a *Frieze* magazine article entitled, 'A Boy's Own Story':

> 'Laddism', he said, 'pretends to be endearingly naughty. Women, faced with lads, are supposed to raise their eyes to heaven in mock despair, thus becoming matriarchal figures who grant their grudgingly but secretly amused blessing ("boys will be boys!") to the sealed male world of laddism. As a heterosexual construct, in which men become little boys with adult desires, and women become their passive but sexually available mothers, laddism is straight from the darker chapters of a psychoanalyst's hand book.'[4]

Correspondingly, as part of our largely-enjoyable discussion about such matters, Jarvis has suggested that:

> 'Success is kind of a manly thing – you have access then to all of the material trappings of a "man". You can get yourself a Rolex watch if you want, and you can get a really fast car,

and hang around with dusky women. If you look at all the things in advertising that seem to represent a successful man, they're pretty childish. I just don't subscribe to that macho idea of what a man is supposed to be'.

Naturally, Jarvis is referencing his opening salvo to 'I'm A Man' – 'Laid here with the advertising sliding past my eyes, like cartoons from other people's lives I start to wonder what it takes to be a man' – although the song's next lyrical skirmish – 'I learned to drink and I learned to smoke and I learned to tell a dirty joke' – tells you everything you need to know on the subject: as much as 'new laddism' was meant to be about irony, Jarvis is having none of it.

'Traditionally, men are more driven to success than women', Jarvis reiterated to Graham Fuller in 1998, 'and if you're successful, that makes you more male, because you're the top dog. But the things that men aspire to remain the same throughout their lives. They play with toys: the Matchbox car becomes the Ferrari. As it says in the song "I'm a Man", if it's all about driving a fast car, then I'm not really interested. I wish there were an alternative manhood. Maybe there is one because I often get referred to as camp. I just think I'm not macho, that's it'.

Musically, 'I'm a Man' is kinda Pixies and kinda grungy, but it's also quite glam – and, yes, Jarvis sounds like the Thin White Duke again – although once the song really starts chug-chug-chugging along, you could be forgiven for thinking you'd walked in on a 1990s shoegazing convention. And perhaps it's this conventional musical landscape that affords the song its charm, a freedom to wear its heart on its sleeve. Much later, in 2009, Jarvis Cocker would release his second solo album, *Further Complications*, and examine the whole *being a man* thing again on songs like 'Homewrecker!' – about a man on the prowl whilst his wife and kids are asleep – and 'Leftovers' – about a man past his sell-by-date employing dreadful puns to chat up women.

'Men are just jerks, aren't they?' Jarvis told Matt Fink for *Under the Radar* magazine in 2009. 'And men never really grow up. Maybe some do. Not all men are jerks. But they're pretty ridiculous, aren't they? Always having to prove themselves, always having to cockfight. Even indie men cockfight. It's still competitive, and I'm part of that. I try to keep a lid on it, but like I say, all those things that are kind of irritating, at least they stop life from being boring. I think that the worst thing, really, is to be bored.'[5]

After one of the song's most profound observations – 'Your car can get up to a hundred and ten, you've nowhere to go but you'll go there again' – 'I'm A Man' signs off with another – 'nothing ever makes no difference to a man, that's what I am' – a sentiment that suggests Jarvis is now resigned to his destiny. Except, we know better, don't we? 'Male models have always got this wide, thick-set, pit bull look to them, with cropped hair and stuff', Cocker told a magazine in 1995. 'To me, that's not a good way for a man to look'. And then, later that year, he'd tell *Attitude* magazine, 'Being skinny is neater and tidier, and it's not got bulges all over. If women were all thin, and men were all muscly, it would be like two different species, like a horse having it off with a tiger.'

Tell that to your average reader of *Loaded*.

13
Let's Get It On

Barry's an odd name, isn't it? Some of my most committed readers will already remember how Barry is a big character on *This Is Hardcore* – Jarvis had collaborated with composer Barry Adamson on 'Set The Controls for the Heart of the Pelvis' whilst the album was being conceived (and, coincidentally, 'Common People' hit the No. 2 spot in the UK the day the song was recorded) and the influence of John Barry is all over the record – and we know how one of the songs was called 'Barry Swings', and that the album could have been called *This Is Barry*.

Of course, in the United Kingdom, the name Barry has associations with . . . what? Sleaze? Ladies' men of the 1970s? Men wearing leather driving gloves when they're chatting up women whilst leaning on the bar in a public house? Some of you, of a more imaginative disposition, might immediately think of Barry White or Barry Manilow, but I just think of Barry Sheen, and Barry from *EastEnders*, or Barry Grant from *Brookside*. That's when I'm not thinking about my sister's ex-boyfriend Barry, who wore Dr. Martens and had a Yamaha FS1E motorbike. Everyone called him Baz.

Along with the title track, 'Seductive Barry' – as on 'The Fear', it features backing vocals by Mandy Bell, Carol Kenyon, and Jackie Rawe – is *This Is Hardcore*'s sleaziest cut, and that's really saying something. Eight and a half minutes in length, and originally operating under the working title 'Sex Symbols', before 'Love Scenes (Seductive Barry)', and then, finally, 'Seductive Barry' took over, the song is about meeting the object of your desires, and how you deal with a fantasy becoming a reality.

> 'Blokes love to look at pictures of naked women in magazines and papers, right?' Jarvis asked Graham Fuller in '98. 'And they say to themselves and each other, "I wouldn't mind giving that some". But if they were actually put in a room with the women in those pictures, they'd probably just blow it, because they wouldn't know what to do. The song's all about having the balls to go through with that situation.'

The *NME*'s Sylvia Patterson subsequently concluded that the song 'sounds a bit like Joy Division; that BIG and bewitching, a sexual fantasy space-pop sequence featuring Jarvis objectifying himself in the eye of the beholder, which then turns into Madonna's "Justify My Love"'.

Elsewhere, 'Seductive Barry' reminds me of 'F.E.E.L.I.N.G .C.A.L.L.E.D.L.O.V.E' and 'My Legendary Girlfriend'. 'I detect the hand of technophile Steve Mackey', we all shout in unison, and indeed Mackey's most persuasively seductive bassline dominates the song. For the record, it's called 'Seductive Barry' because the band thought it sounded like a Barry White song.

'I was singing through a vocoder', Jarvis told Fuller, 'but I didn't have any words for about four or five months. The producer was getting irritated and he kept saying, "When are you going to write some fucking words for this song?" I was worried about it because, I didn't want it to be a re-tread of a song like "My Legendary Girlfriend" or "F.E.E.L.I.N.G.C.A.L.L.E.D.L.O.V.E", which had the same kind of mood. I didn't want it to be like a Barry White song where I'd be saying, "Baby, I'm going to do it to you all night and I'm so fucking hot", and the woman just going, "Yeah, you are". It had to be about meeting on a more even footing, so I came up with the idea of getting a woman's voice to be part of the song instead. That's why we got Neneh Cherry to sing on it'.

Neneh Cherry starts the song off, and is an inspired choice. A collaboration that came about so that the band didn't feel like they were repeating themselves – 'we've done those kind of long, flowing semi-improvised songs before' – Jarvis came up with the idea of not just talking to the woman in the song, or addressing the woman in the song, but the woman actually being there as well.

'I had to think of somebody who was appropriate because I didn't want it to be like Serge Gainsbourg with "Je t'aime"', he told *Raygun*. 'It's very much, "I'm the master of this situation and you just pant, because I'm turning you on so much". So, it needed to be someone that wasn't perceived as a kind of compliant docile woman, do you know what I mean. So, we asked her and she said she'd do it. I was really pleased'.

So utterly postmodern is 'Seductive Barry' that it made me write this sentence. By which I mean to say, how else can you explain lines like, 'Let's make this the greatest love scene from a play no-one's thought up yet'? Ultimately, however, the song reminds me of a Brian De Palma movie – if pushed, I'd plump for *Body Double* or *Dressed to Kill* – featuring Jarvis as the hapless male protagonist, sweating in his attempt at dealing with the movie's displaced love interest. But whilst Cocker and Mackey's obsession with film has been well documented, one wonders why 'Seductive Barry' never made the director's cut in the first place. Before realising, that it already *is* a movie, it's just disguised as a song.

'Seductive Barry's' main claim to fame is that it sounds like we're on the set of a porn movie directed by Jarvis Cocker, starring himself. 'So, roll the soundtrack and dim the lights', he says, and we're not quite sure where to look. We may be used to *Jarvis Cocker: the observer*, but this feels different somehow.

> 'I'm more of a one for observing than instigating', he told *Q* magazine's Phil Sutcliffe in March 1996. 'If you arrange to meet somebody-you're-going-out-with at a train station, it's nice if you can get there early and hide and watch them arrive. I've done that on a number of occasions. You see them the way somebody else would see them. It reminds you of when you first saw them and the way you felt'.[1]

Two years later, whilst listening to 'Seductive Barry', turning up at a train station a bit early sounds kind of *cute* to me.

'Before all this happened', Cocker told the Stud Brothers for *Melody Maker*, as early as 1995, 'I used to walk the streets thinking about what it would be like. I used to dramatize myself. It was like I was starring in my own movie. Everything I did took on this incredibly dramatic perspective. I'd be telling myself stories about myself in my head.'[2]

Presumably, he's not even talking about the usual scarified, stalky, Pulp fare, like 'I Spy' – 'I've been sleeping with your wife for the past sixteen weeks' – or 'Blue Glow' off 1987's *Freaks* album – 'Crouched down by a bush at the roadside I watch as you pass me by' – but instead a future hinterland where Jarvis Cocker is completely in control.

Like a film director.

Like on 'Seductive Barry'.

The hypnotic vocoder effect doesn't help. Once Cocker takes over from Cherry – and that's a phrase I never thought I'd use, as someone not directly involved in the English football league system – with all that 'Here in the night' stuff, it makes you feel like you're in the presence of a stalker, or a predator of some kind. And then we get, 'I don't know where you got those clothes but you can take them off if you feel like it'. It's all very sweet, really, since when you think about it, Jarvis couldn't be anything but sweet if he tried – and he's trying very hard this time. And yet, 'Seductive Barry' successfully delivers a very stark message indeed. *Fame gone wrong?* Tick. *Meeting the object of your desires?* Tick. *One man's fantasy becoming some kind of reality?* Tick, tick, tick.

I think we're all in over our heads here. 'When I close my eyes I can see you lowering yourself to my level', are the first words Jarvis (m)utters to our unseen female antagonist – presumably, this is an acknowledgement of Jarvis's humble socio-sexual standing in front of her, whilst suggesting he's keen to contemplate her breasts at an amenable height discrepancy – and then, barely a few moments later, 'I open my eyes and you're there, even better in the flesh it would seem'. I don't know about you, but as much as I want to imagine our protagonist directing the traffic here, I can't quite get an image out of my head: that of Jarvis sitting on the lap of a lap dancer. *And there's nothing wrong in that,* we all shout from the safety of our sofas, whilst entirely proving my point: Jarvis Cocker as our director/voyeur, as *lapper, and lappee,* is really just a projection of ourselves as hopeless, hapless, fantasists, idealists, *romantics* even. 'I will light your cigarette with a star that has fallen from the sky', he sing-says at one point, and I don't think I've heard anything as innocent, beautiful, beguiling, and *needy* in my life.

But what do I know? I only wandered into this innocent-looking establishment by mistake.

14
You Look Like Her to Me

Finally, a love song! Of sorts. Or rather, 'Sylvia' is a song about something other than pornography.

Or fame.

Or despair.

Hurrah!

'Some people get off on people who they think are a bit screwed up, you know what I mean?' Jarvis reflected on the song. 'I think that's a bit pervy to be honest. This is about a girl who was like that, and it's not the one you think, it's another one. People just wanted to stand near her because she looked right for the room.'

I told you it was a love song.

'Sylvia' may just be about the most traditional song on *This Is Hardcore*, except it's also the most elusive and schizophrenic. 'You look just like Sylvia. Well, you look like her to me', it begins, and we're immediately aware that Sylvia is an *everywoman* Jarvis Cocker has known for so long now that he completely understands everything about her.

So much so, in fact, that he wants to help her.

But haven't we been here before?

Musically, 'Sylvia' is as close to 'Help the Aged' as anything else on *This Is Hardcore* – some of Mark Webber's guitar-playing, particularly in the outro, is reminiscent of Bernard Butler, and the song has elements of mid-1990s Suede, and Radiohead's 'Creep' – but the Sylvia character in 'Sylvia' is surely an updated version of the Susan character in 'Inside Susan', even the unnamed female characters in songs like 'Babies', 'Razzmatazz', and 'I Spy'. 'Who's this man you're talking to? Can't you see what he wants to do?' Jarvis sings at one point on 'Sylvia', and we know immediately that we are on familiar ground: *Jarvis Cocker as Saviour of Women.*

'I suppose you think she's just a silly girl with stupid ideas, but I remember her in those days', sings Jarvis on 'Inside Susan', released as the B-side of 'Razzmatazz' in February 1993, then later that same year as part of *Intro: The Gift Recordings.* Accordingly, 'Babies' – 'Oh, I want to take you home, I want to give you children, you might be my girlfriend'– again stars Jarvis as *Saviour of Women,* whilst 'Razzmatazz' –'You started getting fatter three weeks after I left you' – and 'I Spy' – 'I've been sleeping with your wife for the past sixteen weeks' – are both presumably about revenge against men.

At this point we need to acknowledge that the plethora of female characters that populated Pulp songs in the early 1990s were caricatures of a particular kind of female that Jarvis Cocker had been observing throughout his formative years. There are usually authoritarian, psychologically-abusive men – boyfriends or fathers – on the horizon, or as part of the back story, and in songs like '59 Lyndhurst Grove', in particular – which featured as another 'Razzmatazz' B-side, and as part of the 'Inside Susan' trilogy – Jarvis portrayed himself as both saviour and redeemer.

'[The song was] inspired by a party I'd been to the weekend before', Jarvis told *Record Collector* in 1994. 'We were thrown out by an architect but I got my own back by writing a song about the event. I sent a copy of the CD to 59 Lyndhurst Grove, the lady of the house, because she was in a bad situation married to this prick, but she never wrote back. A Japanese fan went back there and stood outside and asked if she was Susan!'[1]

Interestingly, the sleeve notes for 'Inside Susan: "A story in three songs"' run thus:

. . .following Susan from her Rotherham puberty through wild teen years in Sheffield to her eventual marriage and settling down somewhere on the outskirts of London. I played these songs to Susan the other day – she just laughed and said I was being spiteful because she wouldn't sleep with me when we first met. She also said to tell you that she's perfectly happy where she is at the moment, thank you very much.

Five years on, and by the time we get to the Sylvia character in 'Sylvia', we should be forgiven for thinking that that Japanese fan might just appear at any moment, accusing her of being Susan. Perhaps the line, 'Her father's living with some girl who's a year younger than her', is some kind of pointer in this respect, as is, 'keep believing 'cos you know that you deserve better', since both lines hark back to less sunnier climes, although there's something else going on here, namely, the transformation of Jarvis Cocker from teenager to adult. 'I guess I'm just the same as him, Oh, I just didn't know it then', he reveals at the end of the song, and that lack of self-confidence of yore has gone, replaced by the circumspection of self-loathing.

Sylvia was conceived and recorded in the latter stages of the *This Is Hardcore* sessions, yet it sounds like it could have been off *Different Class*. And it may not be about pornography, fame or despair, so does it even fit on the record? Of course, it does! How else could we know that Jarvis had really grown up?

15
Come Share This Golden Age with Me

I can't pretend that 'Glory Days' is my favourite song on *This Is Hardcore*. To make matters worse, it's not even my favourite song called 'Glory Days', since that particular honour has to go to Bruce Springsteen who had recorded his own 'Glory Days' some sixteen years earlier.

But stop me if you think you've heard this one before. . .

Cocaine 'was around a lot in the Britpop time', Jarvis told the *Glasgow Herald* magazine's Teddy Jamieson in May 2009. 'Initially an interesting thing, 'cos that's a drug that's kind of good for insecure English people. It makes people feel, initially at least, kind of confident, but then after a while it just makes you feel horrible.'[1] A line from 'Glory Days' – 'I did experiments with substances, but all it did was make me ill' – surely references this malaise, but later, as part of the same interview, Jarvis was gracious enough to admit that he was glad he'd lived through Britpop, even though he hated the term.

'I do think it was exciting', he said, 'having lived a marginal life. It did seem like a revolution was possible when indie and underground things began to get mainstream attention. It was like what I'd experienced in the rave scene six years earlier. Again, that was slightly drug induced, but the feeling that socialising could be something other than the aggressive thing it seems to be in the UK – going out and if you can't cop off you smack somebody and if you can't smack somebody you have a curry. It's quite hard work going out in Britain. I don't know how kids do it now.'

Neither do I, but that's beside the point.

Enter 'Glory Days', a song about how kids did it back then. 'Before Tony Blair got elected, they kept ringing me up and asking me if I could count on their support, which I didn't like', Jarvis told Ian Harrison for *Mojo* magazine in December 2006.[2] He continued:

This song 'Cocaine Socialism' came to me one night around that time, in the Groucho Club, when everyone was off their heads from snorting loads of coke. They were probably going to vote Labour, myself included. But it wasn't even champagne socialism any more, it was cocaine socialism and where do socialist principles fit into the most egotistical drug that makes you not give a shit about anyone else? You don't even want to listen to anyone else talk. But I bottled it in the end and rewrote it as 'Glory Days', which was about nothing really.

Damning words, perhaps, but despite the fact that the lyrics for 'Cocaine Socialism' would not survive the song's musical transition to 'Glory Days' – 'Cocaine Socialism' itself would end up as the B-side for the 'A Little Soul' single – the lyrics to 'Glory Days' are surprisingly robust.

Aside from the usual suspects, 'Glory Days' boasts a writing credit for Sheffield-born, occasional Pulp guitarist, Anthony Genn. Genn had originally joined Pulp in January 1988, lasting for six months before he became involved in The Nine 'O' Clock Service, a Sheffield-based Christian cult that incorporated elements of rave culture. In the spirit of serendipity, you should know that Pulp founding member Peter 'Dolly' Dalton also got commandeered by The Nine 'O' Clock Service around this time, and by 1988, I'd already attended a couple of 'services' hoping to 'rescue' him. But it's Genn's official credit for 'additional programming' on *Different Class*, and the fact that he helped out on guitars during some live dates in 1996 and 1997, that suggest his presence on the creative front for 'Glory Days' is not entirely without precedent. The song begins amidst a flurry of elegiac, beautifully-realised piano-bar doodles – featuring Anne Dudley on piano – before the opening lyrical skirmish – 'Come and play the tunes of glory, raise your voice in celebration of the days that we have wasted in the café, in the station' – immediately reminds you of the line, 'Someone left the cake out in the rain', from the 1968 Jimmy Webb-penned hit 'MacArthur Park'. Or maybe that's just me. Either way, there's no denying the enduring appeal of a song that's like a 1990s, Pulpified version of David Bowie's 'Heroes'. Or, come to think of it, isn't it really like something from a '68/'69 Velvet Underground session – 'I Can't Stand It' off *VU*, perhaps? – by which I mean to say, each verse gets relentlessly faster and faster, with barely any sign of a chorus on the horizon.

Just like 'Common People.'

According to the *Melody Maker*'s Robin Bresnark:

Glory Days has it all, that ever-rising tune, Jarvis's hollering voice grabbing for higher and higher stars. It's got the same tirelessly sprinting pace, the same euphoric sense of hope and glory and the same sense of sullied justice as Jarvis sneers: 'We were brought up on the space race, now they expect you to clean toilets.'

Naturally, he's comparing it to 'Common People' – whilst Jarvis is referencing his own childhood dream of wanting to be an astronaut – as did the *NME*'s Sylvia Patterson, who called 'Glory Days' the 'greatest urban hymnal since "Common People" and seems to be, among many other things, about those who live life by the pop star's dictates (and the nutters, perhaps, who thought "Common People" was all about them).'

Incidentally, that comparison to 'Common People' was something that Jarvis was acutely aware of – in the midst of several other anxieties surrounding its original incarnation.

'I had a bit of a phobia about going back to work on "Cocaine Socialism"' he would reveal as part of his essay on the album for the 2006 Deluxe edition, 'because of the psychotic episode it had precipitated but then we found out that the General Election was set for May 1997. If that song was going to come out it had better come out soon. So, we finished it off. And then I said that I didn't want to release it. Now, how the rest of the band restrained themselves from killing me at that point, I don't know – I didn't want to release it because my nerve had gone basically. Yes, I had confused feelings about the Labour Party and yes, maybe it sounded a bit similar to "Common People" but the basic truth was that I didn't have the stomach for it anymore.'

The 'make it up yourself' line has a resigned feel to it – like, *you really want me to do everything for you?* – but elsewhere the song is keen to highlight our contemporaneous generation's lack of *get-up-and-go*, with lines like, 'I could be a genius if I just put my mind to it and I could do anything, if only I could get 'round to it'. That witheringly-reflective line could just as easily have been used in 'I'm a Man', since it's obviously another ironic nod and wink to *Loaded* magazine's modus operandi: '*Loaded* is for the man who believes he can do anything, if only he wasn't hungover.' However, before we get too carried away here, we should be aware that, by this point in proceedings, Jarvis was becoming increasingly irritated at constantly being cast as an ironist.

'That's the thing that I hate', he told Graham Fuller. 'It really irritates me because it implies a detachment and a kind of high-and-mighty viewpoint on things. But all the songs come from real experience, and the only reason I feel I've got the right to write about stuff is that I'm involved in it. And my trying to write about it is a way of trying to make sense of it. I do see little ironies in life, but I haven't got an ironic detachment to my material. If I did, I wouldn't be able to get excited about it'.

Overall, it's very hard to escape 'Glory Days'' bitter grip on reality. For instance, the line, 'Come share this golden age with me in my single-room apartment', manages to be both super-ironic – *look how wonderful my life is! I can't afford a proper house yet!* – and completely authentic. But how could it not be?

'I think a song has to be based on something in real life', Jarvis told his 1,800-strong Brighton Dome audience, as part of his 2008 lecture on the role of lyrics in popular music. 'My girlfriends would sometimes come to our concerts and recognise specific events I mentioned in the songs. But they'd think the rest of the song was real too. In "Common People" the Greek girl really existed but she never wanted to have sex with me. That bit I made up. It's like an iceberg: the top part is based on real life and the rest of it sitting underneath, isn't.'

And that irony thing? Well, it's as good a way as any to smuggle in despair, isn't it? 'Catch me now before I turn to gold', Jarvis mutters towards the end of the song, and then, 'I won't sell these days to anybody else in the world but you', and it's just as witheringly-reflective as everything else on 'Glory Days'. It's almost as if Jarvis has been listening in on our conversations all along, and now he's trying to head us off at the pass.

Infamy, infamy, they've all got in for me.

16
The Meek Shall Inherit Absolutely Nothing at All

Why is 'The Day After the Revolution' the most joyous, perfectly-realised song on *This Is Hardcore*?

Because, it's taken so long to get here, that's why.

But you knew that anyway.

Sometimes, I forget that we're all on the same side.

Twenty years, twenty-one singles (up to 'Party Hard'), and less than a thousand gigs since their formation – I'm not one for hyperbole – Pulp have finally arrived at the precipice. Or, at least, at the end of the road that leads to the junction that leads to the edge of the precipice.

> 'The weirdest thing anyone has said about *This Is Hardcore* so far', Jarvis told *Deluxe* magazine at the time, 'is that the record is really about God. Though, actually, a very strange thing happened when we were recording "The Day After the Revolution" which ought to have, you know, converted me. We knew we wanted it to be quite busy at the end, with a few different voices talking on it, and I got this radio to put a bit of radio noise on it. I couldn't really hear it when we recorded it, so I just stuck it behind the song. When we listened back to it in the studio it was like some

religious broadcast. I honestly hadn't heard it. It's about the creation of the world. Just as the song fades out it says something like, "And God called the expanse sky". And that's it. It was a weird coincidence. And because the song's about maybe a sense of rebirth and this speech is about the creation of the universe, it seemed a bit. . .'

A bit? Well, you know. . .

I can't think of many other finer closing songs to albums than 'The Day After the Revolution'. Okay, I'm going to consider 'Champagne Supernova' off *(What's The Story) Morning Glory* – but not because it says anything about the rest of the record you've just been listening to – and 'Say Yes' off Eliot Smith's *Either/Or*, precisely because it does. And, you've got to have 'Rock 'n' Roll Suicide' off *Ziggy Stardust* and 'The End' from The Doors' eponymous 1967 debut. But other than that, you can argue yourselves stupid about some of the closing tracks off Suede and Radiohead albums – 'The Next Life' off *Suede* and 'Still Life' off *Dog Man Star*, perhaps, and 'The Tourist' off *OK Computer* and 'Street Spirit' off *The Bends* immediately spring to mind – before you end up at, perhaps, the greatest closing track of all time: 'A Day in the Life' off *Sgt. Pepper's Lonely Hearts Club Band*. But 'The Day After the Revolution?' It says it all, doesn't it? I mean, I don't want to say that *This Is Hardcore* was *The Revolution* – or a final reckoning of sorts – but even so.

'The Day After the Revolution' uses an ideal musical template to get its message across: Berlin trilogy-era David Bowie. God, that sounds cynical of me, since, apart from *Station to Station*, *Low*, *Heroes* and *Lodger* are just about my three favourite records of all time. But what all these records have in common is a casual insouciance – both musically and lyrically – like they've seen it all, like they're done with something, like they're *post* something. In Bowie's case, it was post-glam euphoria brought on by drug psychosis. And in Pulp's case, it was probably post-Britpop euphoria brought on by, er, a similar set of circumstances. Or that feeling you get on Sunday when you've spent all Saturday night taking cocaine and ecstasy, so that when it actually gets to Sunday, you've got nothing left to give, it's like you've already lived through Sunday. That's 'The Day After the Revolution', that is.

At one point, Jarvis points out that 'the revolution was televised', directly referencing 'The Revolution Will Not Be Televised', the first song off Gil Scott-Heron's 1971 debut album, *Pieces of My Mind*. Scott-Heron may have written the song after noticing the social unrest and violence in the streets not being reflected on TV, but Jarvis's observation is surely that we're beyond all that – we've seen everything on TV and nothing's changed, nothing will ever change. Yet another line – 'the meek shall inherit absolutely nothing at all' – mirrors 'The Meek Shall Inherit Nothing', off Frank Zappa's 1981 album, *You Are What You Is*, both lines suggesting a state of post-cynicism of epidemic proportions.

Of course, the elephant in the room is the song's apocalyptic finale, where Jarvis suggests that everything is over – including irony! Was Jarvis finally eschewing lyrical irony, the *NME* enquired upon the album's release?

'Well, not wanting to get hung up on the millennium or anything', he replied, 'but I think there's no room for irony when you're entering a new era. There's a kind of desperate need for people to sort themselves out so they're going into a new era with their lives in place. I think that's a good thing. It always got on my nerves anyway when people said Pulp were ironic, because I see the irony in how far short people's lives fall of their aspirations. That is an ironic thing, but the implication is that you're distancing yourself from your subject matter and I never did that. I've only ever been able to write about things that actually mean something to me.'

Later that year, faced with a similar observation from Graham Fuller, Jarvis finally snapped – kind of.

'I'm saying "Stop fucking writing about it", all right?' he said. 'I don't think there's much time for irony in the late '90s as we hurtle toward the new millennium. I think there's a kind of desire around to work things out and there's no point in being detached from such a milestone at the end of the century and the start of the new one, whatever you think of its significance.'

'The Day After the Revolution' is around six minutes in length, but the extended outro featuring a single synthesizer chord pulls it in at around fifteen minutes. The outro is absolutely worth sticking with – not least because it bears out my theory that the song is inspired by Bowie's Berlin trilogy, but also perhaps because it's the only point on the album you could accuse of being *La Monte Young-infused* – although when Jarvis says 'Bye, bye', towards the end, you almost jump out of your skin. Still, if it gets you thinking too long and hard about things you shouldn't be thinking too long and hard about, you should also be aware that *Deluxe* magazine's Vivi McCarthy actually suggested *This Is Hardcore* 'would be music to top yourself to were it not for the euphoric final track "The Day After the Revolution", which recasts Pulp's pop explosion as a mere troublesome dream'. She went on to say, 'It's really Jarvis's honourable farewell to pop as Pulp used to play it. You could not guess what they are going to do after this. According to Mark Webber it might well be Pulp's last record'.

Well, it wasn't, of course, as there would be one more. Following an arena tour of the UK at the end of 1998, Pulp played only another seven shows in the next two years, before releasing the Scott Walker-produced *We Love life* in 2001. But that's another story.

17
"Are you well? Well, you won't be in a minute."

With these ten words, Jarvis Cocker strode on to the stage at an exclusive party at London's Park Lane Hilton Hotel. He had, if you remember, been here before. The date was Wednesday 25 March 1998, and Jarvis was twenty-eight floors above ground level, at the Windows on the World piano bar and restaurant. The party was to mark the imminent release, some five days later, of *This Is Hardcore*, and the band performed a proper Pulp set live with a full line-up for the first time since the V96 Festival – discounting the '*This Is Not A Pulp Gig*' show the previous year – showcasing six new songs, including 'The Fear', 'Dishes', and 'Party Hard', which they'd never played live before, plus 'Help the Aged', 'Seductive Barry' and 'This Is Hardcore', featuring occasional Pulp guitarist Richard Hawley alongside Mark Webber. Martin Green – of London club Smashing notoriety – DJ'd for the night, and for 'Seductive Barry', bassist Steve Mackey took to the record decks. Four hundred guests were invited, and asked to dress in black and pink. I was there, and I can't remember dressing in black or pink, although I do remember Jarvis having a pink handkerchief poking out of his back pocket. At one point, Jarvis introduced, 'Help the Aged' as 'a song about being really immature: It's called "Help the Jarvis"'.

Within days, the critical verdict was in. 'Though the album is less instant, and less instantly classic, than *Different Class*'. commented *The Independent*'s Andy Gill, 'its increased depth pays extra dividends'. 'In midlife oblivion', wrote *Rolling Stone,* 'Pulp have found a strange kind of liberation. Desperation never sounded quite so entertaining'. '*This Is Hardcore* is Pulp on top form', screamed *Q* magazine, 'which is not to say they feel too well.'[1] Finally – finally? – the *NME* concluded that the album was '*Pulp: The Sequel*'.

The following week, however, back when events were being lived rather than re-evaluated, another, perhaps more damning, verdict had come in: *This Is Hardcore* had achieved first-week album sales of just over 50,000, sixty-two per cent fewer than *Different Class*'s first-week sales of 133,000. It took another month before the record was certified gold by the BPI with sales of 100,000, which would have been a triumphant achievement for pre-Britpop Pulp, but in the eyes of the sales-obsessed phenomenon they had helped create, it was a flop – or at the very least a tragic misstep. More than that, it was a death knell for Britpop itself.

By July 1998, Jarvis had taken to agreeing with *Time Out*'s Garry Mulholland that Britpop was just a blip, 'an anomaly. And well and truly over'. *And what of the fame-shattered Jarvis who had started this journey holed up in a Manhattan hotel room on the verge of a mental breakdown?*

'I get the impression', Mulholland suggests, 'of someone having a bit of a row with himself. One side – the "dole-y scumbag", alternative, indie, art-student side – wants art for art's sake, and to be unimpressed by mainstream celebrity. The other – the wrist-flicking, Jacko-taunting, pop-showman side – is a little shocked that the *Different Class* hordes haven't bought into *This Is Hardcore*'s tenser, wordier world.'

To which Jarvis responds: 'There are now two Jarvis Cockers, and the other one is always there and always gives a good performance. Leaving me to get on with being a real person.'

Postlude
The Sound of Failure

"Hello? Is that Mr. Cocker?"

There is a pause, followed by a tentative, *"Ye-es"* from someone on the other end of the line who sounds suspiciously like the man at the heart of this new line of enquiry.

"Grand" says the voice. *"I'll tell you summat for nowt: You're a bloody 'ard bloke to track down, Mr. Cocker. I've been through your record label, a team of unhelpful publicists – one lady was particularly rude, if you don't mind my saying so – and several members of your management team."*

"Who is this?" says someone, who may or may not be Mr. Cocker.

"Oh, Christ!" says the voice. *"I should 'av said. My wife's always on at me: You never introduce yer-self, she says. You always think the world revolves around thee. Well, allow me to introduce me-self. I am the bloke you spoke to in the Philosophy Department of Total Fame Solutions all those years ago!"*

There's a barely perceptible intake of breath – followed by the fumbling sound of someone almost dropping a mobile phone.

"It can't be," says the recipient of this new piece of information. *"The man I spoke to all those years ago had a*

nondescript voice with no regional accent. He was certainly not northern!"

"Well, that was a long time ago," says the voice, "and an awful lot of water's passed under the Hebden Bridge since then! And besides, our Resolutions Department, who've been recording all our calls since time immemorial, recently directed us to sound northern on the phone at all times. Apparently, it puts the caller at ease, makes them open up a bit, you know."

The nature of this worryingly-casual-yet-cynical development in the affairs of TFS is not lost on the other person on the line. And yet he remains silent.

"But all that's beside the point," continues the voice. "I wanted to tell you that our little chat all those years ago 'ad a profound effect on me, and there 'asn't been a day that's gone by when I 'aven't thought about it. Now tell me 'cos I'm dying to know: what did making that record – you know the one you were making back then – tell you about fame and success?"

Our elusive call-recipient thinks for a moment, before attempting to set the record straight.

"Well," he says, "I learned that fame doesn't make you happy! But I knew that anyway. And I also learnt that success is relative. I'm not one for quoting myself, but when we re-released the album eight years after our chat, I said 'in the end, "This Is Hardcore" may be the sound of failure – but it's the most successful rendition of the sound of failure ever put to tape'."

"Nice quote!" says the voice. "But look, fame and success isn't as simple as all that. I think we both agree that fame needs to be earned, and undeserved fame is actually only marginally more palatable than unrecognised fame? Van Gogh only sold* *one painting during his lifetime, and Nietzsche paid publishers to print his works! It is nice to think that those people who deserve our attention and admiration actually receive it as penance for their talent and hard work – but it is not always the case."*

"Mm-hm," our recipient nods in careful agreement.

"And you? Well, I think your initial pursuit of fame was a noble one: you realised that it is impossible to change the world without first being recognised by other people. Surely, without people like you, it is conceivable that the great minds of our time might simply slip through history unnoticed. There's a great quote from Nietzsche: 'Some are born posthumously'!"

"Well, perhaps, I was born post-humorously!" our recipient quips, in a rare attack of whimsy.

The voice makes a noise like a laugh. Although it could just as easily have been a cough or a sob.

"There's something else you need to know," says the voice. *"There is no Philosophy Department at Total Fame Solutions! It was just me all along!"*

There is a sharp intake of breath from our call recipient, as if he has just heard some extraordinarily bad news.

"You all along?" he says, almost wistfully. *"But the Resolutions Department, that's a real thing, right?*

"Oh, yes," says the voice. *"The Resolutions Department is a real thing. You can be sure of that."*

Notes

Chapter 1

1. Maconie, Stuart. 1991. 'Single of the Week.' *New Musical Express*. March 1991.

2. 'Jarvis Tells History.' 1996. *Smash Hits*. 13 March 1996.

3. Mulvey, John. 1996. 'Fiasco 2000!' *New Musical Express*. 2 March 1996.

4. McKie, John. 1996. *The Independent*. 23 February 1996.

5. Mulholland, Garry. 1998. 'The Penetration Game'. *Time Out*. 15 July 1998.

6. Perry, Andrew. 1998. 'The Twilight Zone'. *Select*. April 1998.

7. Barber, Lynn. 1998. 'Puppy Love'. *The Observer*. 5 April 1998.

8. Morley, Paul. 1998. 'Lost and Found'. *Arena*. May 1998.

9. Plummer, Sean. 1998. 'Uncommon People'. *Access Magazine*. May 1998.

10. Hattenstone, Simon. 2008. 'You Can Snort as Much Cocaine as You Want and Have as Many Beautiful Women as You Want . . .But It Doesn't Make You Happy'. *The Guardian*. 24 November 2008.

11. Murison, Krissi. 2020. 'Jarvis Cocker Talks Common People, Parenting and Lockdown without an Audience'. *The Sunday Times*. 11 July 2020.

12. Mossman, Kate. 2021. 'Jarvis Cocker Interview: At the End of 1996, I Had a "a Nervous Breakdown."' *New Statesman*. 20 September 2021.

Chapter 2

1. Simpson, Dave. 1996. 'Fame Fatale'. *Melody Maker*. 30 March 1996.

2. Morris, Gina. 1996. 'Who's Got the Bottle?' *Select Magazine*. August 1996.

3. Jackson, Blair. n.d. 'Producer Chris Thomas: Three Decades on the Cutting Edge and the Charts.' *Mix*. Accessed 1 January 1999.

Chapter 3

1. Smithee, Alan. 1997. 'Out on the Town and Talking Dirty: Jarvis Is Back.' *The Face*. October 1997.

2. Dalton, Stephen. 1998. 'Talking Lewd!' New Musical Express. 28 March 1998.

3. Morton, Roger. 1997. 'New Dentures in Hi-Fi.' *New Musical Express*. 8 November 1997.

4. Sutcliffe, Phil. 1996. *Q Magazine*. March 1996.

5. Sturdy, Mark. 2003. *Truth and Beauty: The Story of Pulp*. Omnibus Press. 2003.

Chapter 4

1. Aldersey-Williams, Hugh. 1998. 'Living Dolls'. *New Statesman*. 8 May 81998.

2. Burgess, Paul, and Louise Colbourne. n.d. *'Hardcore: The Cinematic World of Pulp,'* Thames & Hudson. Accessed 2023.

3. '"They're Not Grotesque – They're Beautiful."' 2003. *The Guardian*. 3 September 2003.

4. Jones, Dylan. 1998. 'Wimpey Bard'. *The Sunday Times Magazine*. 1998.

5. Domanick, Andrea. 2018. 'This Bullshit World Was Predicted by Pulp's This Is Hardcore'. *Vice.* March 20, 2018. https://www.vice.com/en/article/j5agj8/pulp-this-is-hardcore-most-important-album#

6. Colapinto, John. 2015. 'Nabokov's America'. The New Yorker. 30 June 2015.

7. In June 2022, three months after Vladimir Putin's invasion of Ukraine, rumours began to circulate, that the model for the cover of This Is Hardcore, is actually high-profile Russian socialite and model turned TV presenter, Ksenia Sobchak. The daughter of Anatoly Sobchak, the first post-Soviet democratically elected mayor of St Petersburg – and the man who hired KGB officer Vladimir Putin to be his deputy in 1990 – is also rumoured to be Putin's goddaughter. After much research – amidst claims that Zlobina was Sobchak's modelling name – I have found no convincing evidence as to the truth of these rumours.

8. Bresnark, Robin. 1998. 'Sheffield of Dreams'. *Melody Maker*. 27 June 1998.

Chapter 5

1. Sullivan, Caroline. 1998. 'The Friday Review Interview'. *The Guardian*. 27 March 1998.

2. Hornby, Nick. 1998. 'On the Long-Awaited Sequel to Pulp's Breakthrough Album, Different Class, England's Unofficial Laureate Jarvis Cocker Perfects His Poetry of the Prosaic.' *Spin Magazine*. May 1998.

3. McCarthy, Vivi. 1998. 'Confessions of a Pop Star.' *Deluxe*. July 1998.

Chapter 6

1. Krugman, Michael. 1998. 'Deconstructing Jarvis'. *RayGun*. April 1998.

2. Fuller, Graham. 1998. 'Pulp Fiction'. *Interview.* July 1998.

Chapter 7

1. Kot, Greg. n.d. 'Pulp: This Is Hardcore'. *Rolling Stone*. Accessed 23 March 1998.

2. Beaumont, Mark. n.d. '"Like James Bond Playing Strip Poker in a Sex Dungeon": Pulp's This Is Hardcore at 25'. *The Independent*. Accessed 30 March 2023.

3. Patterson, Sylvia. 1998. *New Musical Express*. 21 March 1998.

4. Wilkinson, Roy. 1998. 'Privates on Parade'. *Select.* 1998.

5. Cocker, Jarvis. n.d. '*Mother, Brother, Lover: Selected Lyrics*'. Faber and Faber. Accessed 2011.

Chapter 8

1. Murphy, Peter. 1998. 'Sex, Lies & Videotape'. *Hot Press*. July 1998.

2. Hochman, Steve. 1998. 'Pulp "This Is Hardcore"'. *Los Angeles Times*. 5 April 1998.

Chapter 9

1. Patterson, Sylvia. 1998a. 'Pulp – This Is Hardcore'. *New Musical Express*. 21 March 1998.

2. Hewitt, Ben. 2015. 'Pulp: 10 of the Best'. *The Guardian*. 24 June 2015.

3. Leas, Ryan. 2013. 'The 10 Best Pulp Songs'. *Stereogum*. 8 August 2013.

4. Peschek, David. 2003. *Mojo Magazine*. February 2003.

Chapter 10

1. Cocker, Jarvis. 2008. '*Jarvis on Song: Saying the Unsayable.*' 23 May 2008.

Chapter 11

1. Morgan, Sally. 1998. 'Some Mothers Do Have 'Em.' *Daily Mirror*. 21 November 1998.

2. Eyre, Hermione. 2006. 'The People's Pop Star'. *The Independent on Sunday*. 23 December 2006.

3. Mackinolty, Chips. 2016. 'Mac Cocker, Double J Disc Jockey and Early Advocate of Broadcasting Punk Music'. *Sydney Morning Herald*. 23 June 2016.

4. Ham, Paul. 1998. 'Lost Father Tells Why He Left Jarvis'. *The Sunday Times*. 27 September1998.

Chapter 12

1. Aston, Martin. 1995. 'Jarvis Gets Cocky'. *Attitude Magazine*. November 1995.

2. Phipps, Alison, and Isabel Young. 2012. *'That's What She Said: Women Students' Experiences of "Lad Culture" in Higher Education'*. NUS/University of Sussex. 2012.

3. Lester, Paul. 1995. 'Pulp Diction'. *Melody Maker*. 27 May 1995.

4. Bracewell, Michael. 1996. 'A Boy's Own Story'. *Frieze Magazine*. 1996.

5. Fink, Matt. 2009. 'Jarvis Cocker: Profoundly Shallow'. *Under the Radar Magazine*. 2009.

Chapter 13

1. Sutcliffe, Phil. 1996. 'Common as Muck!' *Q Magazine*. March 1996.

2. Brothers, The Stud. 1995. 'Revenge of the Sex Nerd'. Melody Maker. 4 November 1995.

Chapter 14

1. Reed, John. 1994. *Record Collector*. December 1994.

Chapter 15

1. Jamieson, Teddy. 2009. *Glasgow Herald Magazine*. 2 May 2009.
2. Harrison, Ian. 2006. 'The Mojo Interview'. *Mojo Magazine*. December 2006.

Chapter 17

1. Yates, Robert. 1998. 'Velvet Overground'. *Q Magazine*. 1998.

Acknowledgements

I would like to thank Jarvis Cocker, Steve Mackey, Nick Banks, Candida Doyle, and Mark Webber for making such an incredible record – and Russell Senior for being a part of the band's DNA. Thanks to Chris Thomas for his wonderful production work, Rough Trade's Jeannette Lee and Geoff Travis who have managed Pulp so magnificently over the years, and Peter Saville and John Currin for creating the most beautiful artwork for any album I have ever seen – even though I am in a constant state of confusion and conflict about it.

I'd also like to thank Michele, Kle, Scout and Piper for their continuing support, my amazing editor Ryan Pinkard, as well as the wonderful people at Bloomsbury, particularly Leah Babb-Rosenfeld, and my agent Matthew Hamilton. Also, thank you to Giles Bosworth at Acrylicafternoons.com who consistently provides the best online resource for any band in the world, and the people at PulpWiki. I am also indebted to Paul Burgess and Louise Colbourne for allowing me to quote from *Hardcore* (Volume, 2023) and *Hardcore: The Cinematic*

World of Pulp (Thames & Hudson, 2023), and to Peter Saville for allowing me to quote from his essay therein.

Also, to Mark Sturdy for his excellent Pulp biography, *Truth and Beauty: The Story of Pulp* (Omnibus Press) and Owen Hatherley for his extraordinarily-insightful *Uncommon: An Essay On Pulp* (Zero Books). And I couldn't have written the opening and closing chapters for this book without reading Jed Lea-Henry's brilliant essay, "Audiences for Our Lives: The Philosophy of Fame," and paraphrasing some of Jarvis's thoughts when speaking with Teddy Jamieson for the *Glasgow Herald* magazine in 2009.

Also available in the series

1. *Dusty Springfield's Dusty in Memphis* by Warren Zanes
2. *Love's Forever Changes* by Andrew Hultkrans
3. *Neil Young's Harvest* by Sam Inglis
4. *The Kinks' The Kinks Are the Village Green Preservation Society* by Andy Miller
5. *The Smiths' Meat Is Murder* by Joe Pernice
6. *Pink Floyd's The Piper at the Gates of Dawn* by John Cavanagh
7. *ABBA's ABBA Gold: Greatest Hits* by Elisabeth Vincentelli
8. *The Jimi Hendrix Experience's Electric Ladyland* by John Perry
9. *Joy Division's Unknown Pleasures* by Chris Ott
10. *Prince's Sign "☒" the Times* by Michaelangelo Matos
11. *The Velvet Underground's The Velvet Underground & Nico* by Joe Harvard
12. *The Beatles' Let It Be* by Steve Matteo
13. *James Brown's Live at the Apollo* by Douglas Wolk
14. *Jethro Tull's Aqualung* by Allan Moore
15. *Radiohead's OK Computer* by Dai Griffiths
16. *The Replacements' Let It Be* by Colin Meloy

17. *Led Zeppelin's Led Zeppelin IV* by Erik Davis

18. *The Rolling Stones' Exile on Main St.* by Bill Janovitz

19. *The Beach Boys' Pet Sounds* by Jim Fusilli

20. *Ramones' Ramones* by Nicholas Rombes

21. *Elvis Costello's Armed Forces* by Franklin Bruno

22. *R.E.M.'s Murmur* by J. Niimi

23. *Jeff Buckley's Grace* by Daphne Brooks

24. *DJ Shadow's Endtroducing. . . . .* by Eliot Wilder

25. *MC5's Kick Out the Jams* by Don McLeese

26. *David Bowie's Low* by Hugo Wilcken

27. *Bruce Springsteen's Born in the U.S.A.* by Geoffrey Himes

28. *The Band's Music from Big Pink* by John Niven

29. *Neutral Milk Hotel's In the Aeroplane over the Sea* by Kim Cooper

30. *Beastie Boys' Paul's Boutique* by Dan Le Roy

31. *Pixies' Doolittle* by Ben Sisario

32. *Sly and the Family Stone's There's a Riot Goin' On* by Miles Marshall Lewis

33. *The Stone Roses' The Stone Roses* by Alex Green

34. *Nirvana's In Utero* by Gillian G. Gaar

35. *Bob Dylan's Highway 61 Revisited* by Mark Polizzotti

36. *My Bloody Valentine's Loveless* by Mike McGonigal

37. *The Who's The Who Sell Out* by John Dougan

38. *Guided by Voices' Bee Thousand* by Marc Woodworth

39. *Sonic Youth's Daydream Nation* by Matthew Stearns

40. *Joni Mitchell's Court and Spark* by Sean Nelson

41. *Guns N' Roses' Use Your Illusion I and II* by Eric Weisbard

42. *Stevie Wonder's Songs in the Key of Life* by Zeth Lundy

43. *The Byrds' The Notorious Byrd Brothers* by Ric Menck

44. *Captain Beefheart's Trout Mask Replica* by Kevin Courrier

45. *Minutemen's Double Nickels on the Dime* by Michael T. Fournier

46. *Steely Dan's Aja* by Don Breithaupt

47. *A Tribe Called Quest's People's Instinctive Travels and the Paths of Rhythm* by Shawn Taylor

48. *PJ Harvey's Rid of Me* by Kate Schatz

49. *U2's Achtung Baby* by Stephen Catanzarite

50. *Belle & Sebastian's If You're Feeling Sinister* by Scott Plagenhoef

51. *Nick Drake's Pink Moon* by Amanda Petrusich

52. *Celine Dion's Let's Talk About Love* by Carl Wilson

53. *Tom Waits' Swordfishtrombones* by David Smay

54. *Throbbing Gristle's 20 Jazz Funk Greats* by Drew Daniel

55. *Patti Smith's Horses* by Philip Shaw

56. *Black Sabbath's Master of Reality* by John Darnielle

57. *Slayer's Reign in Blood* by D.X. Ferris

58. *Richard and Linda Thompson's Shoot Out the Lights* by Hayden Childs

59. *The Afghan Whigs' Gentlemen* by Bob Gendron

60. *The Pogues' Rum, Sodomy, and the Lash* by Jeffery T. Roesgen

61. *The Flying Burrito Brothers' The Gilded Palace of Sin* by Bob Proehl

62. *Wire's Pink Flag* by Wilson Neate

63. *Elliott Smith's XO* by Mathew Lemay

64. *Nas' Illmatic* by Matthew Gasteier

65. *Big Star's Radio City* by Bruce Eaton

66. *Madness' One Step Beyond. . .* by Terry Edwards

67. *Brian Eno's Another Green World* by Geeta Dayal

68. *The Flaming Lips' Zaireeka* by Mark Richardson

69. *The Magnetic Fields' 69 Love Songs* by LD Beghtol

70. *Israel Kamakawiwo'ole's Facing Future* by Dan Kois

71. *Public Enemy's It Takes a Nation of Millions to Hold Us Back* by Christopher R. Weingarten

72. *Pavement's Wowee Zowee* by Bryan Charles

73. *AC/DC's Highway to Hell* by Joe Bonomo

74. *Van Dyke Parks's Song Cycle* by Richard Henderson

75. *Slint's Spiderland* by Scott Tennent

76. *Radiohead's Kid A* by Marvin Lin

77. *Fleetwood Mac's Tusk* by Rob Trucks

78. *Nine Inch Nails' Pretty Hate Machine* by Daphne Carr

79. *Ween's Chocolate and Cheese* by Hank Shteamer

80. *Johnny Cash's American Recordings* by Tony Tost

81. *The Rolling Stones' Some Girls* by Cyrus Patell

82. *Dinosaur Jr.'s You're Living All Over Me* by Nick Attfield

83. *Television's Marquee Moon* by Bryan Waterman

84. *Aretha Franklin's Amazing Grace* by Aaron Cohen

85. *Portishead's Dummy* by RJ Wheaton

86. *Talking Heads' Fear of Music* by Jonathan Lethem

87. *Serge Gainsbourg's Histoire de Melody Nelson* by Darran Anderson

88. *They Might Be Giants' Flood* by S. Alexander Reed and Elizabeth Sandifer

89. *Andrew W.K.'s I Get Wet* by Phillip Crandall

90. *Aphex Twin's Selected Ambient Works Volume II* by Marc Weidenbaum

91. *Gang of Four's Entertainment* by Kevin J.H. Dettmar

92. *Richard Hell and the Voidoids' Blank Generation* by Pete Astor

93. *J Dilla's Donuts* by Jordan Ferguson

94. *The Beach Boys' Smile* by Luis Sanchez

95. *Oasis' Definitely Maybe* by Alex Niven

96. *Liz Phair's Exile in Guyville* by Gina Arnold

97. *Kanye West's My Beautiful Dark Twisted Fantasy* by Kirk Walker Graves

98. *Danger Mouse's The Grey Album* by Charles Fairchild

99. *Sigur Rós's ()* by Ethan Hayden

100. *Michael Jackson's Dangerous* by Susan Fast

101. *Can's Tago Mago* by Alan Warner

102. *Bobbie Gentry's Ode to Billie Joe* by Tara Murtha

103. *Hole's Live Through This* by Anwen Crawford

104. *Devo's Freedom of Choice* by Evie Nagy

105. *Dead Kennedys' Fresh Fruit for Rotting Vegetables* by Michael Stewart Foley

106. *Koji Kondo's Super Mario Bros.* by Andrew Schartmann

107. *Beat Happening's Beat Happening* by Bryan C. Parker

108. *Metallica's Metallica* by David Masciotra

109. *Phish's A Live One* by Walter Holland

110. *Miles Davis' Bitches Brew* by George Grella Jr.

111. *Blondie's Parallel Lines* by Kembrew McLeod

112. *Grateful Dead's Workingman's Dead* by Buzz Poole

113. *New Kids On The Block's Hangin' Tough* by Rebecca Wallwork

114. *The Geto Boys' The Geto Boys* by Rolf Potts

115. *Sleater-Kinney's Dig Me Out* by Jovana Babovic

116. *LCD Soundsystem's Sound of Silver* by Ryan Leas

117. *Donny Hathaway's Donny Hathaway Live* by Emily J. Lordi

118. *The Jesus and Mary Chain's Psychocandy* by Paula Mejia

119. *The Modern Lovers' The Modern Lovers* by Sean L. Maloney

120. *Angelo Badalamenti's Soundtrack from Twin Peaks* by Clare Nina Norelli

121. *Young Marble Giants' Colossal Youth* by Michael Blair and Joe Bucciero

122. *The Pharcyde's Bizarre Ride II the Pharcyde* by Andrew Barker

123. *Arcade Fire's The Suburbs* by Eric Eidelstein

124. *Bob Mould's Workbook* by Walter Biggins and Daniel Couch

125. *Camp Lo's Uptown Saturday Night* by Patrick Rivers and Will Fulton

126. *The Raincoats' The Raincoats* by Jenn Pelly

127. *Björk's Homogenic* by Emily Mackay

128. *Merle Haggard's Okie from Muskogee* by Rachel Lee Rubin

129. *Fugazi's In on the Kill Taker* by Joe Gross

130. *Jawbreaker's 24 Hour Revenge Therapy* by Ronen Givony

131. *Lou Reed's Transformer* by Ezra Furman

132. *Siouxsie and the Banshees' Peepshow* by Samantha Bennett

133. *Drive-By Truckers' Southern Rock Opera* by Rien Fertel

134. *dc Talk's Jesus Freak* by Will Stockton and D. Gilson

135. *Tori Amos's Boys for Pele* by Amy Gentry

136. *Odetta's One Grain of Sand* by Matthew Frye Jacobson

137. *Manic Street Preachers' The Holy Bible* by David Evans

138. *The Shangri-Las' Golden Hits of the Shangri-Las* by Ada Wolin

139. *Tom Petty's Southern Accents* by Michael Washburn

140. *Massive Attack's Blue Lines* by Ian Bourland

141. *Wendy Carlos's Switched-On Bach* by Roshanak Kheshti

142. *The Wild Tchoupitoulas' The Wild Tchoupitoulas* by Bryan Wagner

143. *David Bowie's Diamond Dogs* by Glenn Hendler

144. *D'Angelo's Voodoo* by Faith A. Pennick

145. *Judy Garland's Judy at Carnegie Hall* by Manuel Betancourt

146. *Elton John's Blue Moves* by Matthew Restall

147. *Various Artists' I'm Your Fan: The Songs of Leonard Cohen* by Ray Padgett

148. *Janet Jackson's The Velvet Rope* by Ayanna Dozier

149. *Suicide's Suicide* by Andi Coulter

150. *Elvis Presley's From Elvis in Memphis* by Eric Wolfson

151. *Nick Cave and the Bad Seeds' Murder Ballads* by Santi Elijah Holley

152. *24 Carat Black's Ghetto: Misfortune's Wealth* by Zach Schonfeld

ALSO AVAILABLE IN THE SERIES

153. *Carole King's Tapestry* by Loren Glass

154. *Pearl Jam's Vs.* by Clint Brownlee

155. *Roxy Music's Avalon* by Simon Morrison

156. *Duran Duran's Rio* by Annie Zaleski

157. *Donna Summer's Once Upon a Time* by Alex Jeffery

158. *Sam Cooke's Live at the Harlem Square Club, 1963* by Colin Fleming

159. *Janelle Monáe's The ArchAndroid* by Alyssa Favreau

160. *John Prine's John Prine* by Erin Osmon

161. *Maria Callas's Lyric and Coloratura Arias* by Ginger Dellenbaugh

162. *The National's Boxer* by Ryan Pinkard

163. *Kraftwerk's Computer World* by Steve Tupai Francis

164. *Cat Power's Moon Pix* by Donna Kozloskie

165. *George Michael's Faith* by Matthew Horton

166. *Kendrick Lamar's To Pimp a Butterfly* by Sequoia Maner

167. *Britney Spears's Blackout* by Natasha Lasky

168. *Earth, Wind & Fire's That's the Way of the World* by Dwight E. Brooks

169. *Minnie Riperton's Come to My Garden* by Brittnay L. Proctor

170. *Babes in Toyland's Fontanelle* by Selena Chambers

171. *Madvillain's Madvillainy* by Will Hagle

172. *ESG's Come Away with ESG* by Cheri Percy

173. *BBC Radiophonic Workshop's BBC Radiophonic Workshop: A Retrospective* by William Weir

174. *Living Colour's Time's Up* by Kimberly Mack

ALSO AVAILABLE IN THE SERIES

175. *The Go-Go's Beauty and the Beat* by Lisa Whittington-Hill

176. *Madonna's Erotica* by Michael Dango

177. *Body Count's Body Count* by Ben Apatoff

178. *k.d. lang's Ingénue* by Joanna McNaney Stein

179. *Little Richard's Here's Little Richard* by Jordan Bassett

180. *Cardi B's Invasion of Privacy* by Ma'Chell Duma

181. *Pulp's This Is Hardcore* by Jane Savidge